MW00715020

Essential
Mexico

AAA Publishing 1000 AAA Drive, Heathrow, Florida 32746

Original text by Fiona Dunlop
Updated by Anto Howard

American editor: G.K. Sharman

Edited, designed and produced by AA Publishing
© Automobile Association Developments Limited 2008
Maps © Automobile Association Developments Limited 2008

978-1-59508-221-3

Published in the United States by AAA Publishing,
1000 AAA Drive, Heathrow, Florida 32746
Published in the United Kingdom by AA Publishing

Color separation: MRM Graphics Ltd
Printed and bound in Italy by Printer Trento S.r.l.

AO3567
Maps in this title produced from mapping © MAIRDUMONT / Falk Verlag 2007
Mapping data © Footprint Handbooks Limited 2004
Transport map © Communicarta Ltd, UK

About this book

Symbols are used to denote the following categories:

- ✚ map reference to maps on cover
- ✉ address or location
- ☎ telephone number
- ◷ opening times
- ✋ admission charge
- ▮▮ restaurant or café on premises or nearby
- ◙ nearest underground train station
- ◙ nearest bus/tram route
- ◙ nearest overground train station
- ▭ nearest ferry stop
- ✖ nearest airport
- ❓ other practical information
- ℹ tourist information office
- ► indicates the page where you will find a fuller description

This book is divided into five sections.

The essence of Mexico pages 6–19
Introduction; Features; Food and Drink;
Short Break including the 10 Essentials

Planning pages 20–33
Before You Go; Getting There; Getting
Around; Being There

Best places to see pages 34–55
The unmissable highlights of any visit
to Mexico

Best things to do pages 56–75
Good places to have lunch; top
activities; best beaches, places to take
the children and more

Exploring pages 76–185
The best places to visit in Mexico,
organized by area

◆ to ◆◆◆◆ denotes AAA rating

Maps

All map references are to the maps on
the covers. For example, Palenque has
the reference ✚ 21K – indicating the
grid square in which it is to be found

Prices

An indication of the cost of restaurants
at attractions is given by $ signs: $$$
denotes higher prices, $$ denotes
average prices, $ denotes lower prices

Hotel prices

Price are per room per night: $ budget
(under $250 pesos); $$ moderate
($250–$600 pesos); $$$ expensive to
luxury (over $600 pesos)

Restaurant prices

Price for a three-course meal per person
without drinks: $ budget (under $100
pesos); $$ moderate ($100–$150 pesos);
$$$ expensive (over $150 pesos)

Contents

The
essence
of...

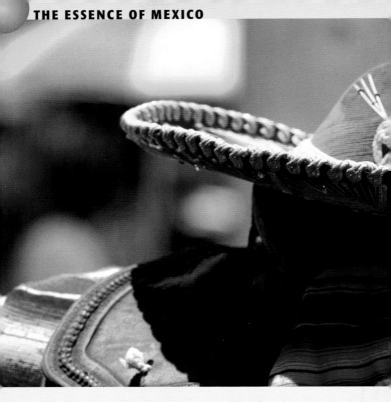

Few nations can rival Mexico's turbulent history, and few can claim such a cultural diversity. From the enigmatic giant heads of the Olmecs and the baroque outpourings of the Spaniards, to the stark clean lines of contemporary architecture and time-honored skills of the craftspeople, Mexico proudly displays a richly creative pulse. Reflecting this are the contrasts of the land itself – tropical rain forests in Chiapas, desert in Baja California, volcanoes and lakes in the center and *cenotes* (sinkholes) in the Yucatán. It is a country that excites, stimulates, and awes. Surprises lurk around every corner.

features

It's hard to avoid clichés when talking about Mexico. It really is a land of contrasts – its people, its climate, its landscape. The majority of Mexicans are *mestizos*, mixed Spanish and Mexican blood, with pure indigenous groups concentrated mainly in the south, in Oaxaca, Chiapas, and the Yucatán peninsula. Other pockets are found in Michoacán (Tarascans), in the mountains of Nayarit and Tabasco (Huichols) and in the rugged northern canyons (Tarahumara).

The official language is Spanish, but the most common native language after that is Nahuatl, the ancient langauge of the Aztecs. The large indigenous populations preserve their own language, customs, dress and crafts, and a visit to a local market makes for a memorable experience. Here you will find a fascinating mix of sights, sounds and aromas and an overwhelming variety of produce and crafts .

GEOGRAPHY
● Mexico's total area is 1,958,201sq km (755,866sq miles), about a quarter of the size of the U.S.A.
● The highest peak is the Pico de Orizaba (5,760m/18,898ft).
● Mexico City lies at an altitude of 2,240m (7,350ft).

- Mexico's coastline totals 10,150km (6,307 miles).
- Mexico is home to nearly 30,000 species of flowering plants, 1,000 species of birds, 2,000 of fish and about 450 of mammals.

SOCIO-ECONOMIC

- Mexico is the world's most populous Spanish-speaking country.
- The population is approximately 100 million, with between 20 and 30 million inhabiting the capital.
- The indigenous population is estimated to be nearly 30 million.
- 56 indigenous languages survive.
- 89.7 percent of Mexicans are Catholics.
- An estimated 45 million Mexicans live in conditions of extreme poverty.

- 1.6 million Mexicans were arrested in 2000 while attempting to cross illegally into the U.S.A.
- 70 years of PRI (Partido Revolucionario Institucional) rule was ended in 2000 when Mexicans voted overwhelmingly for the National Action Party (NAP).

VARIOUS

- There are 200 or so varieties of chili.
- 87 percent of Mexico's tequila exports go to the U.S.A.
- *Pulque*, a pre-Hispanic beer brewed from the maguey plant, still represents about 10 percent of Mexico's total alcohol consumption.

food & drink

Mexican cuisine combines traditional indigenous recipes and ingredients with Spanish and North American influences. As varied as the country's scenery, the food of Mexico covers every budget, from street-corner *tacos* to sophisticated dishes that are reverting to pre-Hispanic recipes after decades of "international" cuisine.

NATIONAL SNACKS

Corn *tortillas* have been the staff of life for centuries, and still accompany most dishes, while *tacos* and *burritos* are stuffed versions that make filling snacks. Less flavorsome wheat *tortillas* are now making inroads in the north, while dark-blue or red versions are made from special types of corn. The ubiquitous *tacos*, sold on every street of the country, are crisp fried *tortillas* stuffed with a fantastic variety of fillings and often topped with grated cheese. If you are careful about where you buy them, *tacos* make delicious and very cheap appetizers. In the south, *tamales* enter the field. These are similar, except that the ingredients are wrapped and steamed in corn husks or banana leaves and may sometimes be sweet. Further variations on the *tortilla* theme include *enchiladas* (cheese or chicken *tacos* baked in a spicy sauce) and *quesadillas*, mainly cheese-filled *tortillas*. A common accompaniment to the above is *frijoles*, red beans in a mushy sauce.

TIMING

To get the most out of Mexican cuisine, follow the Mexican's rhythm. This entails large breakfasts that include fresh fruit and eggs – try *huevos rancheros*, fried eggs and diced chilli in a tomato sauce atop a *tortilla*. Mexican coffee, apart from in the coffee-growing region of Veracruz, is generally a diluted affair, so real aficionados should order espresso, Italian-style coffee is available in most upscale restaurants. Tea is also a pale imitation of the real thing, but Mexicans make up for this with a fantastic selection of fresh fruit juices (*jugos de frutas*), and you can order your own combination.

The main meal in Mexico is lunch, eaten at any time between 2 and 5pm, when restaurants offer good-value set menus (*comidas corridas*). Dinner, if taken at all, is generally after 9pm. Tourists who may not want a large lunch will find that resorts cater to European eating hours, but if you travel off the beaten track you will only find upscale restaurants open in the evenings.

SEAFOOD

Mexican seafood is obviously best along the coast, and resorts cook up exceptionally fresh fish such as *huachinango* (red snapper), *robalo* (snook) and *camarones* (prawn) dishes. However, be warned, *sopa de camarón* is one of Mexico's spiciest dishes. Freshwater fish includes *pescado blanco*, a delicate white fish from Lago de Pátzcuaro, and *langostino*, a large crayfish usually cooked *al mojo de ajo*. This popular seafood preparation consists of fried garlic – again, be warned!

THE ESSENCE OF MEXICO

short break

If you only have a short time to visit Mexico and would like to take home some unforgettable memories, you can do something local and capture the real flavor of the area. The following suggestions will give you a wide range of sights and experiences that won't take long, won't cost very much and will make your visit very special.

● **Stretch out on a Pacific beach** under a shady *palapa* at Huatulco, Puerto Vallarta, or Puerto Escondido, or swim with pelicans and whales in Baja California.

● **Explore a less-visited** archaeological site such as Yagul (➤ 62) to soak up pre-Hispanic history without the crowds.

● **Admire the prowess** of a baroque masterpiece and the fertile imagination of its sculptors in Taxco, Puebla, Cuernavaca, Querétaro, or Oaxaca.

● **Take a boat** tour on a lagoon to observe Mexico's rich bird life, both native and migratory, at San Blas (➤ 137).

● **Get a close-up** of one of Mexico's seismic giants: Popocatépetl, neighboring Iztaccíhuatl, Pico de Orizaba, or the Cofre de Perote, near Jalapa.

THE ESSENCE OF MEXICO

● **Explore the markets** of towns such as
Pátzcuaro (➤ 96) or Oaxaca (➤ 148–152),
where the craft work is outstanding, then tour
the surrounding villages to observe craftspeople
at work.

● **Go scuba diving or snorkeling** at Cozumel
(➤ 176) or Isla Mujeres (➤ 177) in the company
of technicolored tropical fish.

● **Indulge in countless varieties** of tequila at
the Plaza Garibaldi in Mexico City, while being
serenaded by *mariachi* sounds. Do the same
thing in Guadalajara (➤ 92), where the *mariachis*
have their origins, or in Veracruz (➤ 159), where
the *marimba* joins the band.

● **Steep yourself** in colonial history in Mexico City's Centro Histórico, paying homage to the last remnants of the proud Aztec culture at the Templo Mayor (➤ 89), before retreating to a restaurant to sample pre-Hispanic cuisine.

● **Visit an indigenous village** in Chiapas, such as San Juan Chamula (➤ 156), to see a unique synthesis of ancient Maya worship and Catholic rituals.

Planning

Before you go

WHEN TO GO

JAN	FEB	MAR	APR	MAY	JUN	JUL	AUG	SEP	OCT	NOV	DEC
19°C	21°C	24°C	26°C	24°C	23°C	23°C	23°C	23°C	21°C	20°C	19°C
66°F	68°F	75°F	79°F	75°F	73°F	73°F	73°F	73°F	70°F	68°F	66°F

High season   Low season

In Mexico, climate depends as much on altitude as it does on latitude or longitude, so it's difficult to make generalizations. The best time to go is in the dry season, between October and April, but even in the 'rainy season' the rains usually only fall for an hour or two every day. In the northern states it tends to stay relatively dry year round. The highlands, including Mexico City, are usually mild, but with sharp temperature differences between day and night.

August is vacation time for Mexicans and rooms can be scarce in some of the more popular resorts. Día de los Muertos (Day of the Dead) celebrations at the beginning of November are a fun time to see the locals enjoying themselves.

WHAT YOU NEED

● Required   Some countries require a passport to remain valid for a minimum period (usually at least six months) beyond the date of entry – check before you travel.
○ Suggested
▲ Not required

	UK	Germany	USA	Netherlands	Spain
Passport (or National Identity Card where applicable)	●	●	●	●	●
Visa (regulations can change – check before you travel)	▲	▲	▲	▲	▲
Tourist Card	●	●	●	●	●
Return Ticket	●	●	●	●	●
Health Inoculations	▲	▲	▲	▲	▲
Travel Insurance	○	○	○	○	○
Driving Licence (national)	●	●	●	●	●
Car Insurance Certificate (pay extra daily fee for CDW)	○	○	○	○	○
Car Registration Document	●	●	●	●	●

WEBSITES

www.visitmexico.com

www.mexconnect.com

www.mexonline.com

www.mexicocity.com.mx

www.mexperience.com

www.mexicanwave.com

www.sectur.gob.mx

www.cybercaptive.com

TOURIST OFFICES AT HOME

In the U.K.

MexicanTourism Board
Wakefield House
41 Trinity Square
London EC3N 4DJ
☎ 020 7488 9392
Information line: 09065 508917
www.mexicotravel.co.uk

In the U.S.A.

Mexican Tourist Board
400 Madison Avenue
Suite 11C
New York
NY 10017
☎ 212/308-2110
www.visitmexico.com

HEALTH INSURANCE

It is essential to take out a reliable travel insurance policy before leaving home as emergency hospital treatment can be very expensive. For minor ailments pharmacists give good advice, or you can contact a local doctor through your hotel.

Mexican dentists have a very good reputation. If you need emergency treatment, ask at your hotel for a recommendation.

TIME DIFFERENCES

| GMT 12 noon | Mexico City 6AM | Germany 1PM | USA (NY) 7AM | Netherlands 1PM | Spain 1PM |

Mexico has four time zones. Most of the country runs on Central Standard Time (6 hours behind GMT). The northern states of Nayarit, Sinaloa, Sonora and Baja California Sur are on Mountain Standard Time (7 hours behind GMT). Baja California Norte is on Pacific Standard Time (8 hours behind GMT). Quintana Roo (Cancún) is one hour ahead of Central Standard Time. All regions change their clocks in April and October.

NATIONAL HOLIDAYS

Jan 1 *New Year's Day*	*Easter Sunday)*	Oct 12 *Columbus Day*
Feb 5 *Constitution Day*	May 1 *Labor Day*	Nov 1 *All Saints' Day*
Mar 21 *Benito Juárez Day*	May 5 *Battle of Puebla*	Nov 2 *Day of the Dead*
Mar/Apr *Easter (Maundy*	Sep 16 *Independence Day*	Nov 20 *Revolution Day*
Thursday, Good Friday,	*(starting eve of 15)*	Dec 25 *Christmas*

WHAT'S ON WHEN

January Jan 1*: New Year's Day.
Jan 6: Epiphany (Three Kings' Day), celebrated with a special cake.

February Feb 2: Día de la Candelaria.
Feb 5*: Constitution Day.
Shrovetide Carnivals, above all in Veracruz and Mazatlán.

March Mar 21*: Birthday of Benito Juárez.
Mar 21: Spring Equinox festival in Chichén Itzá.
Easter: Palm Sunday*, Maundy Thursday, Good Friday and Easter Sunday*
are the big days. Taxco and the Sierra Tarahumara see the greatest
celebrations. Feria de las
Flores (flower festival) in
Xochimilco on Easter Sunday.

April San Marcos National
Fair in Aguascalientes with
mariachis, bullfights, rodeos.
Late April to early May –
varying dates.

May May 1*: Labor Day.
May 5*: Battle of Puebla (best
in Puebla itself).
Cancún International Jazz
Festival. Varying dates.
Acapulco Music Festival.
Varying dates.

June Feast of Corpus Christi in Mexico City. Varying dates.
Jun 29: Tlaquepaque Festival in Guadalajara. *Mariachis*, dances, parades.

July Third and last Mondays in July: Guelaguetza Festival in Oaxaca.
Music and traditional dances by all Oaxaca's indigenous groups.

August Aug 15: Assumption Day. Streets of Huamantla, Tlaxcala are
carpeted with flower-petal designs.
Mexico City Cultural Festival. Varying dates.

September Sep 15, 16*: Independence Day. Military parades and
festivities nationwide.
President's *grito* on Mexico City's Zócalo.
Sep 21: Autumn Equinox Festival at Chichén Itzá.

October Oct 12*: Día de la Raza (Columbus Day).
Mid- to late-Oct: Cervantino Festival in Guanajuato.
Fiestas de Octubre in Guadalajara. Month-long celebrations with dance,
charreadas, food, arts and crafts exhibits.

November Nov 1: Día de Todos los Santos (All Saints'
Day).
Nov 2: Día de los Muertos (Day of the Dead).
Mexico's fusion of pre-Hispanic and Catholic beliefs
comes to the fore. Renowned celebrations at Pátzcuaro,
Mixquic, Milpa Alta, Iguala. American-style Halloween is
now making inroads on Oct 31.
Nov 20*: Day of the Revolution.

December
Dec 12: Festival of the much-revered Virgen de
Guadalupe. Especially celebrated at the Basílica de
Guadalupe, Mexico City.
Dec 25*: Christmas Day.

* National public holidays when banks and administrative
offices close.

Getting there

BY AIR

Mexico City Airport

13km (8 miles) to city center

🚈 35–45 minutes

🚌 1 hour

🚗 1 hour

Cancun Airport

16km (10 miles) to city center

🚈 N/A

🚌 30–45 minutes

🚗 30–45 minutes

Visitors flying into Mexico have the choice between Mexico City and international airports at beach resorts such as Cancún, Los Cabos, Acapulco or Puerto Vallarta. Guadalajara and Puebla are increasingly popular alternatives. All have money-changing facilities, taxis, restaurants, and duty-free shops.

BY LAND

Arriving in Mexico overland from the U.S. is a popular and relatively easy option. There are several border crossings, and you can park your car on the U.S. side and walk across for a day visit. You also need Mexican automobile insurance to bring in your own vehicle. Most border crossings have long-distance bus terminals, so you can easily get to your destination from the border. You can also cross by land from Guatemala and Belize.

BY SEA

Cruise ships from all around the world dock in Mexican ports. Destinations such as Acapulco, Cozumel, Ensenada and Puerto Vallarta are popular. Contact a travel agent or website such as www.cruiseweb.com for details and schedules.

Getting around

PUBLIC TRANSPORT

Internal flights Domestic and regional airlines in Mexico are not cheap. Aeromexico and Mexicana have the best schedules and deal with bookings for smaller airlines. Mexicana's Mexipass and Mayapass offer considerable savings if bought in your home country.

Trains Mexico's neglected train service is really only viable for overnight trains from the U.S. border to Mexico City or Guadalajara, or between the two towns. An exception is the spectacular Chihuahua–Pacífico route (➤ 36–37). South of the capital, trains are slow, dirty and dangerous.

Buses This is the best way of seeing Mexico on a budget. *Primera* (first-class) long-distance bus services offer excellent value. Each large town has a *Central Camionera* (bus station) with private lines operating different schedules and routes. For trips over 5–6 hours or during public holidays, buy your ticket a day or so in advance. Try to avoid buses where your luggage is stowed on the roof.

Ferries The Mar de Cortés has three ferry routes: La Paz–Mazatlán, Santa Rosalía–Guaymas and La Paz–Topolobampo. The Yucatán peninsula has boats from Playa del Carmen to Cozumel, and Puerto Juárez, Punta Sam (car ferry) or Cancún to Isla Mujeres.

Urban transportation Mexico City's metro is excellent and cheap. *Pesero* buses have their destination marked in front, fares are paid to the driver. Elsewhere in Mexico buses and *colectivos* (collective taxis) are easily available, although each city operates different identification systems. Keep small change handy for fares.

FARES AND CONCESSIONS
Students/youths There is little available in the way of reductions for students, as most youth discounts are for Mexican citizens. Children under the age of 12 get reductions on domestic flights and sometimes free beds in their parents' room.

TAXIS
Mexico City and nearby towns use meters. Elsewhere, a flat fare is charged or price negotiated in advance. Airport taxis and *colectivos* are expensive. At night in Mexico City, use radio-taxi services (☎ 55 5519 7690); taxi-muggings are common.

DRIVING
- Mexicans drive on the right side of the road.
- Seat belts are compulsory for front seats.
- Breath-testing is not widespread in Mexico. Due to widespread drinking, as well as hazards such as cattle and *topes* (speed bumps), it is not advisable to drive at night.
- Fuel is Nova (leaded) or Magna Sin (unleaded) and is sold by the liter. Pemex (Mexican fuel) stations are plentiful in central Mexico, but fill up at every opportunity when driving in less populated areas. Payment is in cash. Fuel stations close by 10pm.
- Speed limits are as follows:
  On highways: 110kph (68mph)
  On country roads: 70–80kph (43–50mph)
  In towns: 40–60kph (25–37mph)
- For any breakdown anywhere in Mexico, contact the Angeles Verdes (Green Angels). This unique service is free and provides on-the-spot technical assistance or tows. Every state has an Angeles Verdes Hotline so it is advisable to obtain this before setting off.

CAR RENTAL
International airports have a large choice of car rental companies. Rates vary considerably. In high season (Dec–Mar) it may be cheaper to reserve from home. A credit card is required to make a deposit. Check the car before signing the contract.

Being there

TOURIST OFFICES
Major state tourist offices
SECTUR
Avenida Presidente Masaryk 172,
Bosque de Chapultepec,
11587 Mexico DF
☎ (55) 5250 0123/5250 0151

Baja California Sur
Coordinación General de Turismo,
Carretera Transpeninsular Km 5.5,
Edificio Fidepaz, Apdo Postal 419,
23090 La Paz, Baja California Sur
☎ (612) 124 0100

Chiapas
Secretaría de Desarollo Turistíco
Blvd Belisario Domínguez 950,
29000 Tuxtla Gutiérrez, Chiapas
☎ (961) 612 4535/613 39396

Guerrero
Acapulco Convention and Visitors
Bureau
Avenue Costera Miguel Alemán
4455, 39850 Acapulco
☎ (744) 484 2423

Oaxaca
Secretaría de Desarollo Turístico
Avenida Independencia 607,
Centro, 68000 Oaxaca, Oaxaca
☎ (951) 515 0717/514 0570

Yucatán
Departamento de Turismo
Calle 59 No 514, Centro, 97000
Mérida, Yucatán
☎ (999) 930 3766

MONEY
The monetary unit of Mexico is the peso ($), divided into 100 centavos.
Coins come in10c, 20c, 50c, $1, $2, $5, and $10 denominations. Notes are
in $10, $20, $50, $100, $200, and $500. Major credit cards (particularly
Visa and MasterCard) are accepted at large hotels, restaurants, travel
agents, and stores. Cash machines are widespread, even in small towns.
International airports all have money-changing facilities with good rates.

POSTAL SERVICES
Correos (post offices) are in every town center and open Mon–Fri 8–6.
Overseas mail is slow but generally reliable, and is a better service than
internal post. Post-boxes *(buzón)* are red, but it is safer to post letters at a
post office. For anything urgent or of value, use a courier service.

TIPS/GRATUITIES

Yes ✓   No ✗

Restaurants (if service not included)	✓	10–15%
Cafés/bars	✓	10%
Taxis	✗	
Tour guides	✓	5–10%
Porters	✓	US$1–$2
Chambermaids	✓	US$1 per day
Toilet attendants	✓	$1 (peso)

TELEPHONES

If possible, bring your own international phone card from home with an access number for Mexico. Otherwise, Ladatel (long-distance) booths are easily found and operate with phone cards (30 pesos, 50 pesos, 100 pesos) bought at local stores. Ladatel offices with operators are also widespread. Avoid making long-distance calls from hotels; taxes increase costs. The country code for Mexico is 52.

International dialling codes

From Mexico to:
U.K.: 00 44
Germany: 00 49
U.S.A. and Canada: 00 1
Netherlands: 00 31
Spain: 00 34

Emergency telephone numbers

Police, fire and ambulance: 080
Green Angels (Tourist patrol): (55) 5250 8221
For other crisis lines, see local phone book.

EMBASSIES AND CONSULATES

U.K. ☎ (55) 5242 8500

Germany ☎ (55) 5283 2200

U.S.A. ☎ (55) 5080 2000

Netherlands ☎ (55) 5258 9921

Spain ☎ (55) 5280 4383

HEALTH ADVICE

Sun advice As in any semitropical country, sunburn is an obvious hazard. Do not sunbathe between noon and 3pm and always use a high-factor sun cream. When visiting archaeological sites, wear a hat.

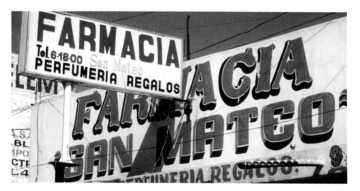

Drugs Prescription and non-prescription drugs are available from pharmacies *(farmacia)*. Bring a basic first-aid kit: mosquito repellent, antihistamine cream for insect bites, a general antibiotic, pain-relief tablets. Anti-malarial treatment need only be taken if traveling extensively in the rainy season (Jun–Sep) near swamps or lagoons.

Safe water and food Never drink tap water. *Agua purificada* (purified water) or bottled water is always supplied in hotels and bottled water is widely available. Drink plenty of water to avoid dehydration. Moctezuma's Revenge (diarrhea) is a common traveler's complaint in Mexico. Avoid eating salads, uncooked or unpasteurized foods (watch out with ice creams) and drinks with ice, except in decent hotels and restaurants. The liberal use of lime juice apparently acts as a deterrent against bacteria.

31

PERSONAL SAFETY

Sensible precautions should be taken, above all in larger cities. Pickpockets operate in crowded areas such as markets and bus stations, so do not tempt them by exhibiting jewelry, cameras, or thick wallets. Do not leave valuables lying around in your hotel room; use a safety deposit box. Muggings are on the increase in Mexico City (➤ 28, Taxis) so do not carry anything other than essentials. Elsewhere, avoid taking solitary walks in remote areas or driving after dark. If anything is stolen, report it for insurance purposes.

ELECTRICITY

The power supply is 110 volts. Sockets use two-flat-pin plugs (U.S. style), so Europeans need an adapter and transformer. Most mid- and upper-range hotels have universal outlets for shavers.

OPENING HOURS

- ● Shops
- ● Banks
- ● Casa de Cambio
- ● Museums/Monuments
- ● Pharmacies

In hotter areas and coastal resorts, shops close at 1 or 2 for lunch, reopening at 4–5pm and finally closing around 9pm.
Certain banks operate longer hours than above.
Post offices open Monday to Friday 8–6.
Street markets start at 7am.
Museums are generally closed on Mondays, and there are regional variations to the opening hours.

LANGUAGE

Spanish is the language used throughout Mexico, although in large resorts English is widely spoken. If traveling to smaller places it is essential to know a few basic phrases. Mexican Spanish has slight differences in vocabulary and usage from Castillian Spanish, but otherwise is very similar. Accents change throughout this vast country, and in some areas you will hear local indigenous languages such as Náhuatl, Maya or Zapotec.

Hello! Good morning	*Hola! Buenos días!*	Please/thank you	*Por favor/gracias*
Good afternoon	*Buenas tardes!*	It's a pleasure	*De nada*
Good night	*Buenas noches!*	I don't speak Spanish	*No hablo español*
Goodbye/see you	*Adiós/hasta luego*	Do you speak English?	*¿Habla inglés?*
Yes/no	*Sí/no*		
Do you have a single/double room?	*¿Tiene una habitación sencilla/doble?*	For two nights	*Para dos noches*
		With fan/air-conditioning	*Con ventilador/aire acondicionado*
With a balcony/sea view	*Con balcon/vista al mar*	Is there a swimming-pool	*¿Hay una alberca?*
How much does it cost?	*¿Cuánto cuesta?/ Cuánta se cobre?*	Do you take credit cards?	*¿Accepta tarjetas de crédito?*
Very expensive/cheap/too much	*Muy caro/barato/ demasiado*	Where is the nearest bank?	*Dónde esta el banco mas cerca?*
Can I have the menu/bill, please?	*El menu/la cuenta, por favor*	A cup of black coffee with milk	*Un café americano/ con leche*
We'll have two beers please	*Dos cervezas por favor*	Fruit juice	*Un jugo de fruta*
Fizzy mineral water	*Un agua mineral*	A bottle of red/white wine	*Una botella de vino tinto/blanco*
Where is the bus station?	*¿Dónde esta el central camionera?*	How far is the nearest petrol station?	*¿A qué distancia esta la gasolinera mas cerca?*
Straight on/to the left/to the right	*Todo derecho/a la izquierda/a la derecha*	How long is the journey?	*¿Cuánto tiempo dura el viaje?*

Best places to see

1 Barranca del Cobre

Rugged canyons, spectacular waterfalls, old mining villages, Jesuit missions, and the Chihuahua-Pacifico railroad are the highlights of the Copper Canyon.

Five times wider and one-and-a-half times deeper than the Grand Canyon, the 35,000sq km (13,510sq miles) Barranca del Cobre is rapidly becoming a major ecotourism destination. It is composed of five adjoining canyons sliced out of the Sierra Madre Occidental, their sculpted ravines offering startling extremes in climate and vegetation. In winter the upper plateau may be blanketed in snow, while on the canyon floors warm, balmy temperatures prevail; in summer the Sierra Tarahumara is refreshingly cooler than oven-like Chihuahua, though rain is abundant.

The most striking access to this region is by rail, through 88 tunnels and over 39 bridges from Los Mochis, near the Mar de Cortés, to Divisadero and Creel, or arriving in the other less scenic direction from Chihuahua. The main town is Creel. Facilities here include day trips on horseback or by van into the surrounding canyons, to Lago Arareco, Cascada de Cusararé, the hot springs of Recohuata or the six-hour ride to Batopilas, a former silver-mining town 2,000m (6,560ft) below on the canyon floor. In the far north are the thundering waters of the Cascada de Basaseáchic, a 246m (807ft) waterfall whose spectacular pine-clad surroundings are now a national park.

The original inhabitants of this region, the Tarahumara, now only number about 50,000. Their geographical isolation has preserved their distinctive traditions that climax during colorful Easter processions.

✚ 6D 🚆 Daily 1st- and 2nd-class train leaves Los Mochis at 6am, Chihuahua at 7am ✈ Airports at Los Mochis and Chihuahua ❓ Easter processions and dances peak on Easter Fri
ℹ Libertad 1300, 1st Floor, Edificio Agustín Melgar, Chihuahua

2 Chichén Itzá

This archaeological site is the most popular in the Yucatán peninsula. Two distinct excavated zones present extraordinary and unique structures.

Founded in AD514 by a priest, this ceremonial center experienced two peaks, from 600 to 900, and again from the late 10th century until 1196. Civil wars and cultural stagnation followed before Chichén and other northern Maya civilizations finally collapsed in 1441. When the Spaniards arrived a century later, they named the partially ruined structures according to mere supposition.

At the center of the vast plaza in the northern group rises the striking Pyramid of Kukulkán (El Castillo). Its 365 steps and 52 base panels represent the solar year, and twice a year, at the spring and summer equinoxes, the shadows of the north staircase create a serpentine shape that joins the carved snakes' heads at the bottom. To the northwest is a ball court, the largest yet discovered in Mexico, lined with bas-reliefs of players. Overshadowing this is the Templo de los Jaguares (Temple of Jaguars), with extensive jaguar and eagle carvings. Beside it stands the macabre Tzompantli (Platform of Skulls), that once displayed the heads of sacrificial victims.

Across the plaza is the richly decorated Templo de los Guerreros (Warriors' Temple) with, at its base, an extensive, roofless colonnade, the Mil Columnas (Thousand Columns). From the platform high above, the entire plaza is surveyed by a much-photographed *chacmool* (seated human figure).

The highlight of the older group is the Caracol (snail), an elevated circular building once used for astronomical observations. Facing it is the ornately decorated Edificio de las Monjas (nunnery) and, between them, the Iglesia (church), crowned by a remarkable roof comb and adorned with masks of the rain god, Chac.

✚ 23H ☎ (985) 851 0137 ⊙ Site and museum: daily 8–6; services: 8am–10pm ♿ Expensive; moderate Sun
🍴 Cafeteria ($) 🚌 ADO bus from Mérida, Calle 50
❓ Sound and light show nightly: 8pm in Spanish; 9pm in English. Spring and fall (autumn) equinox celebrations
ℹ Tourist information offices in Mérida and Cancún

3 Guanajuato

www.guanajuato.gob.mx

Tumbling down a hillside in central Mexico is this gem of a town. Former silver wealth has left a legacy of superb colonial architecture.

Historically one of Mexico's most important towns, Guanajuato originally earned its status from its rich silver mines, founded in 1546. It never looked back and in 1989 was declared a world heritage site by UNESCO. A network of underground tunnels keeps traffic out of its central plazas and alleys, making it a joy to wander in, though less so to drive in as orientation is not easy.

On a hilltop overlooking the town are the old mines of La Valenciana (one still functions), next to a 1770s church containing three fine baroque altarpieces. Further along the Carretera Panorámica is the Museo de las Momías, another of

Guanajuato's unique sights, containing over 100 mummified bodies retrieved from the local cemetery where they had been impeccably preserved in the mineral-rich soil.

In the town center, the main attraction is the **Alhóndiga de Granaditas,** which houses the regional museum. This imposing building, originally a corn exchange, played a major role in the War of Independence when it became a fortress and later the macabre showcase for the heads of captured rebels. It now exhibits pre-Hispanic objects, altarpieces, religious paintings, and items related to the Independence struggle. A short walk east brings you to the grandiose University, one of the most important in Mexico and, just beyond, the Templo de la Compañia de Jesús, a 1750s church with a remarkable facade. Immediately below is the focal point of town, the lively Jardín de la Unión, backed by the highly decorative Teatro Juárez.

✚ 15H ✖ Flights from Mexico City

ℹ Plaza de la Paz 14 ☎ (473) 732 1982

Alhóndiga de Granaditas

✉ Calle 28 de Septiembre ☎ (473) 732 1112 ⬤ Mon–Sat 10–2, 4–6, Sun 10–3. Closed Dec 25, Jan 1, Easter Sun

4 Huatulco

www.baysofhuatulco.com.mxi

Situated on what was once a deserted coastline, this fledgling resort offers dramatic scenery and excellent services.

Although Huatulco's string of nine bays was spotted by the Spanish conquistadores, they were never exploited as a port. For centuries, this idyllic fishing village slumbered peacefully before being earmarked in the early 1980s by Mexico's resort planners as a follow-up to Cancún. Progress was not always smooth; development suffered from the 1994–5 financial crisis and Hurricane Pauline in 1997. However, unlike other Pacific resorts, planners have learned from their mistakes elsewhere and built an environmentally sensitive resort with low-rise hotels.

Today, Huatulco boasts an international airport, over 20 hotels, a marina, an 18-hole golf course and three developed beaches at Tangolunda (the most exclusive), Santa Cruz, and Chahue, as well as a lively inland village, La Crucecita, with budget accommodation. Other beaches remain blissfully untouched with, at the most, a few *palapa*

restaurants. Between the pockets of hotels are jungle-clad hills and cliffs that are rich in wildlife. Activities include jungle motorbike expeditions, kayaking, snorkeling, and diving around the reefs in Huatulco's clear waters.

Although historical sights are totally absent, Huatulco boasts a modern *zócalo* at the center of La Crucecita. This animated hub is overlooked by a church, **Iglesia de Guadalupe,** worth visiting for its vast contemporary mural of the Virgen de Guadalupe that decorates the entire ceiling vault.

✠ 19L ✖ Flights from Oaxaca, Mexico City
🛈 Santa Cruz, corner Monte Albán, Bahía de Santa Cruz
☎ (958) 581 0176/0177
Iglesia de Guadalupe
✉ Calle Gardenia, La Crucecita 🕐 Daily 9–8 🍴 Cafés and restaurants ($–$$) on plaza

5 Monte Albán

"White Mountain" sits atop a leveled hill above the valley of Oaxaca. Magnificent in scale, layout and setting, it is an absolute must-see.

Incredible 360-degree views of the barren hills surrounding Monte Albán give a strong sense of proximity to the gods, a fact recognized by the later Mixtecs, who used the abandoned site for offerings and burials between 1350 and the arrival of the Spaniards. The ancient Zapotec site was founded around 500BC and peaked between AD500 and 600 with an estimated population of over 20,000. Like many other Mesoamerican sites, it was abandoned in the 8th century and, apart from its Mixtec interlude, fell into ruin.

From the site entrance and well-designed museum, a path winds uphill to the corner of the northern pyramid, where the breathtaking Gran Plaza opens up before you. To the left is a ball court, a palace, and small temple platforms, and opposite are three large temple structures. Between them a 300m (985ft) plaza unfolds to the majestic steps of the southern pyramid. Other buildings are aligned down the center, yet the overall sense of space remains absolute from any vantage point.

Behind the northern pyramid are five tombs, the most elaborate being Tomb 104. East of this, near the access path, is Tomb 7, source of the fabulous Mixtec treasures displayed in Oaxaca's museum. On the western flank of the plaza, the Palacio de los Danzantes (Palace of the Dancers) was named after a series of stone slabs carved with dancing figures that stand around its base. There are countless theories about these oddly deformed figures.

➕ 18L ✉ 6km (4 miles) west of Oaxaca ☎ (951) 516 1215
🕐 Daily 8–5 ✋ Moderate
🍴 Café ($) on site 🚌 Buses from Oaxaca, Calle Mina 518, every 30 mins 8:30–3:30 ✈ Numerous internal flights to Oaxaca
ℹ Sedetur: Independencia, corner García Vigil, Oaxaca
☎ (951) 516 0123

6 Museo Nacional de Antropología

www.mna.inah.gob.mx

This museum is a must for any visitor to Mexico City, as it houses an exemplary display of the nation's indigenous cultures.

Built in the early 1960s, the Anthropological Museum does full justice to the complexities of

MUSEO NACIONAL DE

Mexico's early civilizations through a dynamic display grouped according to regions. The focal point is a large semi-roofed courtyard fountain; surrounding it are the ground-floor galleries devoted to Mesoamerican artifacts and the upper floor to the rich diversity of surviving traditions among Mexico's indigenous populations. Another attraction is the museum's verdant location in Chapultepec Park, offering a leafy post-museum walk.

The ground-floor galleries start in the right-hand wing and follow a counterclockwise direction around the courtyard. An introduction to world anthropology and ethnology continues with the origins of the Mesoamericans, before moving into pre-Classic civilizations (1700–200BC). Then follow rooms dedicated to Teotihuacán, Tula (the Toltecs), México (the Aztecs), Oaxaca (Mixtecs and Zapotecs), the Gulf of Mexico (Olmecs, Huastecs and Totonacs), Maya, northern desert cultures, and finally Occidente (the western cultures of Nayarit, Jalisco, and Colima). After visiting some of the archaeological sites covered, the museum collection becomes far more relevant and illuminating.

Highlights include the giant Toltec *Atlante* statue in the Sala de Tula, the Aztec Calendar stone in the spectacular Sala México, and a huge Olmec head from San Lorenzo. Other notable exhibits are the superb Olmec *luchador* (wrestler), the Mayan mask of the Sun God, reproductions of Mayan murals from Bonampak, and a reconstruction of King Pakal's tomb from Palenque.

🕂 *Ciudad de México 1d* ✉ Paseo de la Reforma, corner Gandhi, Bosque de Chapultepec, Mexico City ☎ (55) 5553 6386/6381 🕒 Tue–Sun 9–7 ✋ Moderate 🍴 Café ($) off courtyard 🚇 Chapultepec ❓ Guided tours, audio-guides, bookshop

7 Palenque

Deep in the rainforest of Chiapas stands this superb Maya site, both evocative and historically significant.

Palenque was founded in AD615 by the great Mayan king Pakal, who set out to create a new architectural style. At the center of the main site stands the Palacio (palace), a large complex of courtyards, corridors and tunnels crowned by a tiered tower that was probably an observatory. The entire structure is decorated with relief carvings, stucco friezes, and carved stelae.

Virtually opposite towers the Templo de las Inscripciones (Temple of Inscriptions), where steep steps rise to a summit temple then descend into the extraordinary tomb of King Pakal. Over 620 hieroglyphic inscriptions (including the date of 692) are surrounded by rich stucco decoration. Pakal's carved sarcophagus remains in the crypt but his fabulous jewelry is now at Mexico City's Anthropological Museum (➤ 46–47). Temple XIII, immediately to the west, has revealed the entombed body of the Reina Roja (red queen), adorned with fine jade ornaments that are at the site museum.

Across a stream on the hillside is a group of four beautiful temples. Some distance north lies another distinct group where a ball court fronts the Templo del Conde (Count's Temple). From here a path leads along the stream through jungle and past unexcavated structures to the main road and the museum and crafts shop.

🚑 21K ☎ (916) 345 0356/0211 🕐 Daily 8–5 ✋ Moderate
🍴 Cafeteria ($) in museum 🚌 Collectivo bus to site from
Calle Allende, Palenque ✈ Airstrip ❓ As these ruins are in
a remote location, check with your hotel for any local
developments that may affect your safety
ℹ Avenida Juárez, corner Absolo, Palenque

Taxco

Taxco boasts a spectacular natural setting high in pine-covered mountains and some impressive colonial extravaganzas.

Taxco, a former staging-post on the royal road south to the port of Acapulco, developed considerably in the 18th century thanks to the enterprising French mining magnate José de la Borda, who left his mark both here and in Cuernavaca. A subsequent long and somnolent period ended in the 1930s when the American William Spratling regenerated the silver industry.

Red-roofed, whitewashed houses tumbling down the slopes line a maze of crooked cobblestoned streets winding uphill from the main road to the Plaza Borda. This social and commercial hub is overshadowed by the magnificent church of **Santa Prisca** (1759), a baroque masterpiece that was entirely financed by Borda. No expense was spared; its ornately carved facade and towers house a dazzling interior lined with 12 gilded altarpieces, oil paintings and a monumental organ.

On a tiny plaza behind the church, the Museo Guillermo Spratling exhibits pre-Hispanic artifacts and replicas. A few twisting steps downhill from here stands a museum honoring another of Taxco's illustrious foreign residents, the German explorer Baron von Humboldt, who lived here in 1803. His mansion now houses the Museo de Arte Virreinal, a beautifully presented collection of colonial art with some exceptional pieces. There are numerous other fine mansions and churches to be explored, and a lively market area in the streets below Santa Prisca, packed with silver stores, offers the joys of hard bargaining.

Finally, for panoramic views of the town from the summit of Monte Taxco, take the *teleférico* (cable-car) from Los Arcos, located on the main access road.

➕ 16K ❓ Easter Week processions peaking on Easter Fri
ℹ️ Avenida de los Plateros 1 ☎ (762) 622 6616
Parroquía de Santa Prisca
✉️ Plaza Borda ☎ (762) 662 0183 ⏰ Mon–Sat 6am–8pm, Sun 5:30am–9pm 🍴 Cafés and restaurants ($) on square

9 Teotihuacán

Long before the Aztecs established their capital in central Mexico, Teotihuacán was the dominant center.

Located an hour's drive from Mexico City, the archaeological site of Teotihuacán ("place of the dead") rises out of dry scrub and cacti. This once magnificent city, that covered over 20sq km (8sq miles) and sustained some 85,000 inhabitants at its zenith, evolved over a period of eight centuries before its destruction around AD750. Controversial 20th-century excavations and restoration of about 80 percent of the structures highlight Teotihuacán's ambitious building, carving and mural techniques.

The site lies a few degrees off a north–south axis traced by the Avenue of the Dead, that ends at the magnificent Pirámide de la Luna (Pyramid of the Moon). At the southern end is the vast Citadel, a walled quadrangle with the Temple of Quetzalcóatl against the eastern wall. This astonishing stepped construction (around AD200), later built over, honors the plumed serpent (Quetzalcóatl) and the rain god (Tláloc) with 366 stone carvings.

Further north looms the gigantic Pirámide del Sol (Pyramid of the Sun) and, in its southern shadow, a dramatically designed and enlightening new museum displaying priceless exhibits and a huge scale model of the site, crossed by a transparent walkway. At the northwest end of the avenue, flanking another large ceremonial area, stands the extensively restored Palacio de Quetzalpapálotl, part of the priests' residential complex. Here, on an elevated patio, are square columns carved with bird and butterfly designs and remnants of red wall friezes. More patios and lower chambers show depictions of the jaguar god, conch shells and birds. A climb to the summit of the Pirámide de la Luna offers a final, sweeping view of this once great city.

➕ 17J ☎ (55) 5956 0052 🕐 Daily 7am–6pm ✋ Moderate 🍴 Restaurant ($) opposite the Citadel 🚌 Pirámides' bus from Terminal Tapo 🚇 San Lázaro ❓ Guided tours from Mexico City (through hotels, travel agents)
ℹ️ SECTUR: Avenida Presidente Mazariyk 172, Polanco, Mexico City

10 Xochimilco

Xochimilco is a throwback to the capital's Aztec origins, with its canals and "floating" nursery gardens.

On the far southern edge of Mexico City, weekends are an excuse for feasting on fresh air while cruising the verdant canals of Xochimilco to the insistent tunes of *mariachis*. Brilliantly decorated, pole-propelled *trajineras* (Mexican gondolas), packed with large groups or families, combine with countless flower- and food-sellers in canoes to create watery traffic jams. But this is Mexico, and chaos is part of the colorful picture.

The tradition of "floating" gardens goes back to the Aztecs, who, due to a shortage of farmland, devised a method of creating islands rooted by willow trees. These *chinampas* were used to grow fruit, vegetables and flowers to supply Tenochtitlán, the capital.

Xochimilco covers an area of 135sq km (52sq miles) that includes the town itself, with its beautiful 16th-century church of San Bernardino de Siena, beside several others, an archaeological museum, and the Parque Ecológico, an extensive area of grasslands, lagoons and canals. This is an ideal destination for birdwatchers, families or anyone desperate for unpolluted air close to the city center.

Xochimilco's final offering is a fascinating private **museum** housed in an atmospheric 400-year-old hacienda. The vast landscaped grounds are an added draw. Named after its owner, Dolores Olmedo, the museum exhibits an important collection of paintings by Diego Rivera and his wives, Frida Kahlo and Angelina Beloff, as well as pre-Hispanic artifacts (some probably copies) and an impressive collection of folk art.

✚ 17J 🐾 Moderate 🚇 Tren Ligero: La Noria, from Tasqueña 🚢 Fixed boat prices at Embarcadero ❓ Two-hour tours available (in Spanish) of Parque Ecológico ☎ (55) 5673 8061/7890 or in English through travel agents

Museo Dolores Olmedo Patiño
✉ Avenida México 5843, La Noria ☎ (55) 5555 1221/0891 🕐 Tue–Sun 10–6 except Dec 25, Jan 1 and Easter Sun 🍴 Pleasant open-air café ($)

Best things to do

Good places to have lunch

Beto's Condesa ($$)

Popular beachfront restaurant where you have the tantalizing choice between lobster and succulent steaks.

✉ Playa Condesa, Costera Miguel Aleman, Acapulco ☎ (744) 484 0100/0473

Caesar's ($$)

Bustling seafood restaurant in the center of Loreto.

✉ Emiliano Zapata, corner Benito Juárez, Loreto ☎ (613) 133 0203

Café del Bosque ($$)

Lakeside restaurant in Chapultepec Park. Mexican and international dishes with live *marimba* music.

✉ Off Paseo de la Reforma, Bosque de Chapultepec, Mexico City
☎ (55) 5515 4652/5516 4214

Café la Gloria ($$)

In the arty, leafy quarter of Colonia Condesa. Informal, popular lunch spot with outdoor tables serving international cuisine. Young, colorful clientele.

✉ Vicente Suárez 41, corner Amatlan, Colonia Condesa, Mexico City
☎ (55) 5211 4180

Casa Oaxaca ($$$)

Some of the most creative food in Southern Mexico is created at this modern, romantic eatery. Fish is the house specialty. Not to be confused with Casa Oaxaca Hotel's own restaurant.

✉ Constitución 104A, Oaxaca ☎ (951) 516 8889

El Anclote ($–$$)

Flee to the northernmost headland of Bahía de Banderas for the ultimate beachside lunch. Seafood soup, beef, chicken or fresh lobster.

✉ Playa El Anclote, Punta Mita, Puerto Vallarta ☎ (322) 222 1949

El Tule ($$$)

Panoramic hotel restaurant on the hillside. Regional specialties and international cuisine.

✉ Hotel Victoria, Lomas del Fortin 1, Oaxaca ☎ (951) 515 2633

Gran Café del Portal ($$)

A Veracruz institution, founded in 1810 as La Parroquia. Breakfasts extend into lunches; much favored by local dignitaries.

✉ Independencia, corner Zamora, Veracruz ☎ (228) 932 9339

La Casona ($$)

Beautifully restored mansion with attractive patio and garden for cool lunches. Italian cuisine.

✉ Calle 60, No 434, Mérida ☎ (999) 923 8348

♦♦ La Bella Italia ($)

Sunny garden courtyard for devouring delicious Italian dishes away from shopaholic crowds.

✉ Canal 21 Col Centro, San Miguel de Allende ☎ (415) 152 4989

Top activities

Cenote **diving** in the Yucatán Peninsula

Diving in the Caribbean at Los Manchones, off Isla Mujeres

Horse-back riding in Baja California's Sierra de la Giganta or in the hills around Oaxaca

Kayaking across the Bahía de Banderas, off Puerto Vallarta

Parasailing at Acapulco, Ixtapa, Cancún or Puerto Vallarta

Playing golf at the top 18-hole course designed by Jack Nicklaus at Cabo del Sol, Los Cabos

Rocking along in the Chihuahua–Pacífico Copper Canyon train

Swimming with dolphins on Isla Mujeres or on Cozumel

Watching the divers at La Quebrada, Acapulco

Whale-watching (Dec– Apr) in Baja California

in the Oaxaca Valley

This drive covers the valley southeast of the state capital, taking in craft villages and archaeological sites.

Leave Oaxaca by following signs to Istmo or Tehuantepec, which brings you to Highway 190. You soon enter the village of El Tule, with its colorful church and giant tree.

This gnarled ahuehuete tree is claimed to be the world's largest tree, standing 40m (130ft) high and weighing an estimated 550 tons. It is thought to be some 2,000 years old and is still sprouting.

Continue 6km (4 miles) on the highway to a turn-off on the right to Tlacochuaya.

Here a magnificent church stands within a Dominican monastery complex, its interior notable for ornate floral murals and a 16th-century organ.

Return to the highway, continue east, stopping at the archaeological site of Dainzú before turning left to Teotitlán del Valle, famed for its bright wall-hangings and hand-woven rugs (tapetes). Return and continue along the highway to another turn-off on the left to Yagul.

This little-visited Zapotec site sits high in the cactus-studded hills and offers fabulous 360-degree views of the valley. Its ball court is the second largest in Mesoamerica.

Follow the highway to an intersection, take the left fork to Mitla. Drive into the village plaza.

Visit the Frissell Museum before walking uphill past numerous crafts outlets to the red-domed church, crafts market and the superb Zapotec structures (➤ 154).

Continue east from Mitla to a turn-off to Hierve del Agua. An unsurfaced road leads to this sensational site – a petrified mineral waterfall and pools. Return to Oaxaca by the same route.

Distance 120km (75 miles)
Time 5–6 hours, depending on stops
Start/end point Oaxaca ✚ 18L
Lunch Centeotl ($) ✉ Zona Arqueológica Yagul ☎ (951) 562 0289

Best souvenirs

Day of the Dead masks from towns throughout Tlaxcala state

Decorative tinwork from Oaxaca

Handblown glass from Tonalá, Guadalajara

Handmade hammocks from Mérida and the rest of the Yucatán

Handwoven textiles from Chiapas and Oaxaca

Jade jewelry from Michoacán

Laca, or lacquerware, from the state of Guerrero

Leather goods from the ranching towns of northern and central Mexico, such as Durango and Zacatecas

Silver jewelry and tableware from Taxco

Talavera ceramics from Puebla or cheaper look-alikes from Dolores Hidalgo

Architectural gems

Capilla del Rosario in Puebla's Santo Domingo (➤ 96)

Catedral Metropolitana in Mexico City (➤ 82)

Catedral de Zacatecas in Zacatecas

Palacio de Bellas Artes in Mexico City (➤ 87)

Parroquía de San Miguel in San Miguel de Allende (➤ 100)

Santa Clara and **Santa Rosa** in Querétaro (➤ 100)

Santo Domingo in Oaxaca (➤ 152)

Santo Domingo in San Cristóbal de las Casas (➤ 156)

Santa Prisca in Taxco (➤ 50–51)

Templo de la Valenciana in Guanajuato (➤ 40)

Best climbs

Iztaccíhuatl, the sister volcano to Popocatépetl, for a close-up on Popo's rising steam (➤ 17)

The church of **Nuestra Señora de Los Remedios,** atop the largest pyramid in the Americas at Cholula (➤ 90)

The **Pirámide de la Luna** at Teotihuacán for a clear view of early town-planning (➤ 52, 53)

Cheat at Taxco and take the cable-car up to **Monte de Taxco** (➤ 51)

The giant statue of Morelos on the **island of Janitzio** overlooking Lago de Pátzcuaro (➤ 96)

El Faro (the lighthouse) at Mazatlán, the world's second-highest natural lighthouse after Gibraltar (➤ 136)

The dunes at **El Faro Viejo** in Cabo San Lucas, for panoramic ocean views (➤ 123)

Nohoch Mul at Cobá, the tallest pyramid on the northern Yucatán peninsula, for sweeping jungle views (➤ 173)

The **Torre Latinoamericana** in Mexico City: another cheat as you'll be in an elevator (➤ 89)

El Castillo, at the heart of Chichén Itzá (➤ 38–39)

Places to take the children

Acuario Mazatlán
Over 50 aquariums with 200 species of fish from all over the world, performing sea lions, a marine museum, and theater.
✉ Avenida de los Desportes 111, behind Motel del Sol, Mazatlán
☎ (669) 981 7815 🕐 Daily 9:30–6

Africam
Impressive project that re-creates the environment of Africa to preserve and breed endangered species. Also children's zoo and restaurant.
✉ Km 16.5, Carretera Valsequillo, Puebla 🕐 Daily 10–5 🚌 Bus 72 from Boulevard Heroes del 5 de Mayo, Puebla

Aquaworld
Cancún's largest watersports centre has an underwater "sub see explorer" that glides through coral reefs for a dry close-up of marine life. Also jungle tours, snorkeling and diving lessons.
✉ Km 15, Boulevard Kukulcán, opposite Melia Hotel, Cancún
☎ (998) 848 8327 🕐 Daily 6:30am–10pm

CICI
Aquariums, dolphins, and water rides keep children more than happy at this well-established park.
✉ Costera Miguel Alemán, Acapulco ☎ (744) 484 8210
🕐 Daily 10–6

Dolphin Discovery
Swim with dolphins on Isla Mujeres. Well organized but reservations essential. Minimum age 8 years if accompanied by adult, 12 years if not. Day trips from Cancún, ferry leaves from Playa Langosta.
✉ Playa Langosta, Isla Mujeres ☎ (998) 883 0777/0779 🕐 Four swims daily at 9, 11, 1 and 3

El Nuevo Reino Aventura

Southern Mexico City's answer to Disneyland, with over 45 rides, games, a dinosaur show, and other attractions.

✉ Carretera Picacho–Ajusto 1500, Mexico City ☎ (55) 5645 0559 🕓 Tue–Thu 10–6, Fri–Sun 10–7 Ⓜ Taxqueña or Universidad, then taxi

Wet 'n Wild

Toboggans, water slides, waterchutes and several pools designed for young children. Snorkeling and diving, restaurants, bars, and shops.

✉ Km 25, Boulevard Kukulcán Cancún ☎ (998) 885 1855 🕓 Daily from 9am

Xcaret

Vast seaside development with endless attractions – Mayan temples, underground rivers, aquarium, swimming with dolphins, horse-back riding, aviary, butterfly pavilion, orchid farm, museum.

✉ 8km (5km) south of Playa del Carmen, on Highway 307 ☎ (998) 883 3143/883 3144 🕓 Daily 8:30am–10pm

Yumka

Huge jungle and wetlands park with 30-minute boat tour or train through African-type savannah. Good children's attractions.

✉ Camino a Yumka, 16km (10 miles) from Villahermosa ☎ (993) 356 0107 🕓 Daily 9–4

Zoológico Miguel Álvarez del Toro

Fabulous zoo where over 200 Central American species roam in large, natural enclosures. Jaguars, quetzals, tapirs, toucans, and more on the outskirts of Tuxtla.

✉ Off Libramiento Sur Oriente, Tuxtla Gutiérrez ☎ (961) 614 4701 🕓 Tue–Sun 9–5

Peace and quiet

Mexico's diverse topography offers a bewildering choice of escapes for those in search of a return to nature. Hand-in-hand with the rainforest, sierras, scrub, pine forests, desert, and volcanic craters goes a varied wildlife, from iguanas, harpy eagles and quetzals to jaguars, Jesus Christ lizards, and grey whales.

Savannah, sea and *cenotes*
Visitors to the Yucatán peninsula should explore the Sian Ka'an Biosphere Reserve to see the savannah edging mangrove swamps and, on the horizon, the world's second-longest ocean reef. Pumas, white-tail deer, crocodiles, howler monkeys and some 300 bird species are all resident, best observed on a trek organized through Amigos de Sian Ka'an, in Cancún. On the north and west coast respectively, Río Lagartos and Celestún reserves are favorite nesting grounds for pink flamingos, and the tiny island of Isla Contoy (➤ 177) remains a rewarding bird sanctuary.

Jungle wilds
Most of Mexico's original rain forest is concentrated in Chiapas, where high rainfall helps maintain steamy jungles, much appreciated by macaws, toucans, parakeets, spider monkeys, and butterflies, and mammals such as jaguars and ocelots. Montes Azules is the most accessible ecotourism destination in this region. Mexico's largest cloud forest is at El Triunfo Biosphere Reserve, near Tapachula in the Sierra Madre range.

Coast to hills
Beyond the Isthmus, in the state of Oaxaca, the land becomes noticeably drier. Nature-lovers should enjoy the diving facilities at Puerto Escondido and Huatulco. Here, too, are coastal wetlands such as the Lagunas de Chacahua and the turtle sanctuary of Mazunte. In stark contrast, the area around Catemaco (southeast of Veracruz) is dubbed "little Switzerland," while in Tabasco there are more coastal lagoons as well as savannah and jungle.

Volcano territory

Central Mexico is the land of the volcanoes. The national park surrounding the twin peaks of Popocatépetl and Iztaccíhuatl, the crater lakes of Nevado de Toluca, and the more strenuous ascent of Pico de Orizaba all offer extensive hiking and climbing. The Michoacán village engulfed by the seismic activity of Paricutín in the 1940s offers a striking spectacle and can be explored on a horseback tour from Uruapan.

Desert

Endless scrub, sierra and desert characterize most of northern Mexico, with notable exceptions provided by the spectacular canyons of the Sierra Tarahumara and the coastal lagoons between Mazatlán and San Blas. The biosphere reserves of the islands in the Mar de Cortés have a spectacular 570 species of plants and the sea itself over 15 species of whales and porpoises. In Baja California, the Sierra de la Gigánta and the Desierto de Vizcaíno are home to puma and lynx, as well as exceptional desert landscapes and flora.

Best beaches

Playa de las Ánimas, south of Puerto Vallarta, is a pretty, serene beach near a tiny fishing village where you can get some great fresh seafood.

Playa Delfines in Cancún offers a good view of the turquoise Caribbean.

Playa Hornitos, in Acapulco, is often overcrowded and thus a little uncomfortable, but it has to be experienced at least once for the high-energy, beautiful people vibe.

Playa Mazunte, 13km (8 miles) west of Puerto Angel, is a stunning stretch of soft sand with a few simple and very tasty seafood joints nearby.

Playa Miramar, an isolated beach south of San Blas, is popular with surfers and seekers of solitude.

Playa Norte, on Isla Mujeres, has shallow, calm, turquoise waters that are perfect for a relaxing dip between sunbathing sessions.

Playa Palancar, on Cozumel, is the resort island's most overlooked beach, with famous off-shore Palancar Reef for diving and a few hammocks hanging under coconut palms inviting an afternoon snooze.

Playa La Ropa in Zihuatanejo, surrounded by palm trees, fronts a calm bay that draws sailboats and sand-soccer players alike.

Tulúm, 130km (80 miles) south of Cancún, has a tiny cove below the Mayan ruins edged with white sand that is one of the most picturesque beaches in Mexico. You can hike from the ruins down to the beach for a refreshing dip in the water; bring a swimsuit.

Zipolite, 60km (37 miles) east of Puerto Escondido, is a backpacker's favorite with its cheap accommodations and chilled-out crowd.

Exploring

Traveling through Mexico can be a strangely familiar experience because so much of it has clear European and North American influences. But behind this hybrid facade lies the more secret life of the indigenous people, whose ancestors erected the most incredible pyramids and structures.

Traditional crafts reflect the imagination and flair of the Mexicans, whether intricate handweavings, touchingly crude Tarahumara animal carvings, exquisite ceramics and silverware, or tin *milagros* (votive offerings to saints).

Mexico's magnificent Spanish heritage is one of dazzling baroque masterpieces and grid-like urban layouts, with the inevitable *zócalo*, the social crossroads of every town. In contrast, as the northern border draws closer, there is a distinct feel of growing prosperity and increasing Americanization.

Central Mexico

Central Mexico is the volcano-studded heart of the nation's colonial heritage. It was the silver mines of Zacatecas and Guanajuato that financed countless cathedrals in Spain, while a stream of baroque masterpieces was created in a roll-call of towns from Cuernavaca to Querétaro, Morelia and Puebla.

For today's conquistadores, this is not only one of the most culturally rewarding regions, where interest ranges from local craft specialties to exceptionally designed museums and dramatic archaeological sites, but it also offers spectacular scenery, lakes, forests, and generally cooler temperatures. Political events have marked this region – Morelia was the birthplace of José María Morelos, one of the leaders of the Independence movement, and the state of Morelos was the battleground of Emiliano Zapata, the revolutionary hero.

Mexico City

Vibrant, ever-expanding and highly polluted, Mexico City is the political, cultural and economic heart of the country. Rimmed by volcanoes and lying at an altitude of 2,240m (7,350ft), Mexico's capital now claims over 20 million inhabitants. All of them surrender to the precariousness of living in a city that is sinking into the underground Lago de Texcoco, is plagued by crime and yet survived the terrible earthquake of 1985 with incredible civic solidarity. But despite all its negative factors, no one should pass up on a chance to spend a few days in this stimulating megalopolis.

Mexico City (Ciudad de México) can be divided into three main zones of interest – the Centro Histórico and Alameda area; the Zona Rosa and Chapultepec; and, far to the south, San Angel, Coyoacán, and Xochimilco. From Aztec ruins to impressive colonial edifices interspersed with modern blocks and wide boulevards, it presents strong visual contrasts. And between these facades cruises a stream of traffic, monopolized by the ubiquitous Volkswagen "beetles", the mainstay of the taxi business. In the Centro Histórico, pedicabs have been introduced, offering an alternative, more leisurely form of transport, while the excellent metro system covers the entire city.

Finding your way around can be frustrating, but the streets, alive with color, noise, and activity, more than compensate for this.

🚩 17J

ℹ️ Avenida Presidente Masaryk 172 ☎ (55) 5250 0123/5250 0151

BOSQUE DE CHAPULTEPEC

This extensive park marks the western limits of the city center and is a favorite with some half-a-million city dwellers for weekend walks, picnics, and spontaneous open-air entertainment. Lakes, woods, lawns, museums, an amusement park, a zoo, and restaurants are among its diverse offerings. An entire day can easily be spent here.

Crowning the hill is the 1785 Castillo de Chapultepec, which houses the **Museo Nacional de Historia.** Here, a rather dusty display covers Mexican history, and there are murals and the sumptuous royal apartments of the hapless Emperor Maximilian and his wife, Carlota. Don't miss the sweeping views from the terrace café. The castle is reached by a winding path from the Monumento a los Niños Héroes (Monument to the Young Heroes), at the main park entrance, which passes the snail-like Museo del Caracol (covering Independence and the Revolution) on the way.

The star of Chapultepec is the Museo Nacional de Antropología (➤ 46–47), located on the busy Paseo de la Reforma that slices across the park. Nearby are two major art museums – the Museo de Arte Moderno, and the Museo Rufino Tamayo (which concentrates on temporary exhibitions of contemporary art). Further west lies the Jardín Botánico, boating lakes, restaurants, a high-tech children's museum – **Museo del Papalote** – an amusement park, and the zoo that claims to be the world's oldest, as it existed during Aztec rule.

✚ Ciudad de México 1e

Museo Nacional de Historia

☎ (55) 5516 2848 🕒 Tue–Sun 10–5 💰 Inexpensive; free Sun 🍴 Café ($) on premises 🚇 Chapultepec

Museo del Papalote

✉ Avenida Constituyentes, Bosque de Chapultepec ☎ (55) 5237 1781 🕒 Daily 9–1, 2–6 🚇 Constituyentes

CATEDRAL METROPOLITANA

Dominating the *Zócalo*, Mexico City's main historic square, is this massive cathedral (Latin America's largest), which was begun in 1563, although its baroque facade dates from 1681 and the asymmetrical towers and dome were added in 1813. The walls incorporate stones from the ruins of the Aztec Temple of Quetzalcóatl, but far more visible is the gilded baroque of the Capilla de Los Reyes (Chapel of the Kings) that glows in the gloomy interior. Subsidence is an ongoing problem – note the slope from high altar to the entrance – and metal structural supports are unfortunately highly visible. Next door stands the Churrigueresque-style El Sagrario (The Sacred), with a remarkably ornate facade dating from 1760.

✚ *Ciudad de México 8c (off map)* ✉ *Zócalo*, Centro Histórico
🕐 Daily 7–7 🖐 Free 🍴 Cafés ($) on main square 🚇 *Zócalo*

MUSEO ANAHUACALLI

This outstanding museum is unfortunately located on the far southern edge of Coyoacán and requires some effort to visit. Conceived by the famous muralist and artist Diego Rivera, it embodies his identification with Mesoamerican culture. The pyramidal lava-stone structure houses his collection of 60,000 pre-Hispanic artifacts and a studio where he worked briefly before his death in 1957, leaving some unfinished paintings. Dark, labyrinthine corridors with onyx windows, stone ceiling mosaics, open terraces, arches, and stepped, altar-like displays all echo pre-Hispanic forms.

✠ *Ciudad de México 4f (off map)* ✉ Calle del Museo 150, San Pablo de Tepetlapa ☎ (55) 5617 4310 🕔 Tue–Sun 10–6. Closed Holy Week 💰 Moderate; free Sun 🚇 Taxqueña, then taxi

MUSEO DEL CARMEN

On the edge of the delightful residential area of San Angel, in a cloistered garden, is this former Carmelite monastery, built in 1617 with tiled domes. The attractive, unusual interior encompasses floral friezes, wood and gesso ceiling reliefs, tiles, and frescos. Displayed throughout the former chapels and cells is an important collection of baroque religious art and, in the crypt, a somewhat ghoulish line-up of mummies.

✠ *Ciudad de México 4f (off map)* ✉ Avenida Revolución 4, San Angel ☎ (55) 5616 2816 🕔 Tue–Sun 10–5 💰 Moderate 🍴 Cafés/restaurants ($–$$) on Plaza San Jacinto 🚌 San Angel *pesero* bus down Insurgentes

a walk through San Angel

A wander through the relaxed neighborhood of San Angel, along tree-lined cobbled streets, takes in ancient churches, museums, and shops.

From the San Angel pesero bus terminal walk up Avenida Revolución to the Museo del Carmen (▶ 83) on your right. After visiting this monument, cross the avenue to the Centro Cultural and walk along Calle Madero to Plaza San Jacinto, lined with shops and restaurants.

On the right-hand side, the 18th-century Casa del Risco offers an unusual ceramic and shell-encrusted fountain, while inside it displays 16th- to 18th-century Mexican and European art. Next door is the Bazar del Sábado, a large crafts market open only on Saturdays. On the far corner of the plaza stands the beautiful 16th-century church and former monastery of San Jacinto.

Continue along this street, past the crossroads, when it becomes Calle Miguel Hidalgo. At the 17th-century Casa Blanca turn right into Licenciados, following it downhill into Calle Leandro Valle.

These quiet streets offer a classic vision of Mexico City's wealthier residences, often brightly painted and set behind high walls, in a wide range of architectural styles.

At the main crossroads cross Altavista, passing a beautiful 18th-century hacienda on your left (now the San Angel Inn). Opposite stands the Museo Estudio Diego Rivera.

This blue structure was designed in 1930 for Rivera and includes a smaller, adjoining structure intended for Frida Kahlo. Rivera's studio, where he died in 1957, gives a fascinating insight into his last years.

Walk east down Altavista to Avenida Revolución and the Museo de Arte Carrillo Gil opposite, before returning south to the bus terminal.

Distance About 3km (2 miles)
Time 2–3 hours, depending on stops
Start/end point San Angel bus terminal
Lunch Restaurant Antigua San Angel Inn ($$$; ➤ 105)

MUSEO FRANZ MAYER

Opened in 1986 in a superbly restored 16th-century mansion, this museum contains an exceptional collection of 16th- to 19th-century fine and applied arts amassed by German immigrant and construction magnate, Franz Mayer. Influences and contrasts are highlighted between Asian, Middle Eastern, European, and Mexican styles, and priceless exhibits include paintings by Velázquez, Rivera, and Zubarán. Inlaid furniture, tapestries, silver and gold objects, wooden sculptures, glass, and ceramics complete this impressive collection.

➕ *Ciudad de México 8b* ✉ Avenida Hidalgo 45, Colonia Guerrero ☎ (55) 5518 2266 🕐 Tue–Sun 10–5 💲 Moderate 🍴 Café del Claustro ($) 🚇 Hidalgo, Bellas Artes

MUSEO FRIDA KAHLO

Deep indigo and red-ochre walls picked out with brilliant green window-frames announce the eclectic and flamboyant tastes of Mexico's foremost woman artist, Frida Kahlo. Located in the pretty tree-lined streets of Coyoacán, where she spent most of her life, her family home reflects her wide-ranging interests and obsessions, and includes some poignant items such as the wheelchair to which she was confined in her last years, her four-poster bed and her last, unfinished painting (a portrait of Stalin). Beside these is a wealth of memorabilia in which Kahlo's husband, the artist Diego Rivera, figures strongly, alongside her collections of masks, Teotihuacán sculptures, ex-votos, glass, lacquerware, and ceramics.

✚ *Ciudad de México 4f (off map)* ✉ Calle
Londres 247, Coyoacán ☎ (55) 5554 5999
🕐 Tue–Sun 10–6 ✋ Moderate 🍴 Cafés,
restaurants ($–$$) on Jardín Centenario
Ⓜ General Anaya, then taxi

MUSEO NACIONAL DE ANTROPOLOGÍA

Best places to see, pages 46–47.

PALACIO DE BELLAS ARTES

Another of Mexico City's architectural showstoppers presides over
the lively park, Alameda Central, on the western edge of the

Centro Histórico. The Bellas
Artes is a popular cultural center,
with excellent temporary
exhibitions, a theater where the
Ballet Folklórico performs, a
bookshop, gift shop, restaurant
and a display of murals by
Rivera, Orozco and Siqueiros
alongside Tamayo, on the upper
floors. Set around a vast marble-
lined atrium, the interior is pure
art deco, in total contrast to the
exuberant domed and
colonnaded exterior.

✚ *Ciudad de México 8c* ✉ Corner
Avenida Juárez and Eje Central,
Centro ☎ (55) 5512 2593 🕐 Palace:
daily 10–6; museum: Tue–Sun 10–6
✋ Free 🍴 Café del Palacio ($$)
Ⓜ Bellas Artes ❓ Ballet Folklórico:
Wed, Sun mornings and Sun evenings

PALACIO NACIONAL

Mexico's first parliament is housed within this vast edifice flanking the eastern side of the *Zócalo*. The 17th-century palace replaced two previous ones, and is still the political powerhouse of Mexico as it holds the offices of the President, the National Archives and the Federal Treasury. Above the main entrance hangs the symbolic "Freedom Bell" that rang out in the town of Dolores, on September 15, 1810 to announce the fight for Independence. This is rung annually on the eve of Independence Day by the president to teeming masses gathered in the square.

Inside the courtyard a grand staircase leads up past extensive murals by Rivera, a tour de force that covers the history of Mexico. It is well worth following a guide to have the endless details explained. A small museum on the second floor is dedicated to Mexico's most revered president Benito Juárez.

✚ *Ciudad de México 8c (off map)*
✉ *Zócalo* ☎ (55) 9158 1259
🕐 Mon–Sat 9–6, Sun 9–2 🖑 Free, but bring identification 🍴 Cafés ($) on Zócalo 🚇 Zócalo ❓ Military lowering of flag daily before sunset with brass band

TEMPLO MAYOR

On the northeastern corner of the *Zócalo* is one of the few Aztec sites that remain. When it was completed in 1487, the temple consisted of seven superimposed structures, each one involving a four-day dedication ceremony and several thousand sacrificial victims. It was unearthed by accident in 1978 during construction of the metro. Four years of excavations uncovered hundreds of superb sculptures, housed in a museum behind the site, designed to resemble the temple layout. Visitors can wander through the temple ruins on raised walkways that give close-ups on the altars devoted to Tláloc, god of rain, and Huitzilopochtli, god of war, along with replicas of sculptures. Highly visible is the wall of skulls in front of the museum, while inside, one of the most outstanding exhibits is a huge carved stone disc depicting the dismembered goddess of the moon, Coyolxauhqui.

➕ *Ciudad de México 8c (off map)* ✉ Seminario 8, Centro ☎ (55) 5542 4784 🕐 Tue–Sun 9–5 👆 Moderate 🍴 Restaurants ($–$$) in and near Zócalo 🚇 Zócalo

TORRE LATINOAMERICANA

This lofty downtown landmark was the capital's first skyscraper when completed in 1956, but has since been surpassed by others. Towering 139m (456ft), it survived the 1985 earthquake and other tremors due to ingenious anti-seismic foundations that incorporate 361 concrete stilts. Today, it offers the best vantage point for views over the city (on rare, smogless days), particularly breathtaking at night. On the 44th floor is an outdoor viewing deck.

➕ *Ciudad de México 8c* ✉ Corner Avenida Madero and Lázaro Cárdenas ☎ (55) 5512 0844 🕐 Daily, 9:30am–10:30pm 👆 Moderate 🍴 Cafés and restaurants ($–$$) in Centro Histórico 🚇 Bellas Artes, San Juan de Letrán

XOCHIMILCO

Best places to see, pages 54–55.

More to see in Central Mexico

CHOLULA

Once a major ceremonial town dedicated to Quetzalcóatl, Cholula suffered extensive destruction by Cortés' army on its march to Mexico City. Numerous shrines and churches include the Convento Franciscano (1549) and the 18th-century Capilla Real with its 49 domes. The **Gran Pirámide,** the largest pyramid in the Americas, dominates this otherwise nondescript town. Crowning the summit is the 16th-century Templo de Nuestra

Señora de los Remedios (Temple of Our Lady of Remedies), while below, some 8km (5 miles) of tunnels have revealed extensive remains of murals. A small museum near the tunnel entrance houses copies of the frescos.

✚ 17K ❓ Guides available to explore main tunnel

ℹ Opposite main entrance

Gran Pirámide

✉ Highway 190, Cholula 🕓 Daily 10–5

✋ Moderate; free Sun 🍴 Restaurant Choloyán ($), Avenida Morelos

CUERNAVACA

Often dubbed the "city of eternal spring," Cuernavaca is a favorite get-away spot for the capital's wealthier inhabitants. Despite a population of over one million, and the largest number of swimming pools per capita in the world, it has a delightful center, and, situated only 65km (40 miles) south of Mexico City, makes an attractive alternative base. Two adjoining plazas form the heart of town, over which looms the **Palacio de Cortés** (1530), a massive fortress-palace housing a fascinating museum of regional archaeology, colonial history, and the Revolution. There is also a masterful mural by Diego Rivera depicting Spanish oppression of the indigenous peoples.

In front lie the plazas, focal points for a crafts market, promenading, and general festivities. A short walk west up Calle Hidalgo brings you to the magnificent Catedral (1530), built by the Franciscans. Despite being one of Mexico's oldest churches, its interior is strikingly modern. Across Avenida Morelos is the Jardín Borda, a beautiful landscaped garden surrounding a mansion (1783) built by French silver magnate José de la Borda. It was once a favorite retreat for Emperor Maximilian. Historical documents, folk art, and temporary art shows are among the exhibits.

✚ 17K

ℹ Avenida Morelos Sur 187, Colonia La Palma ☎ (777) 318 7561

Palacio de Cortés

✉ Avenida Benito Juárez ☎ (777) 312 8171 🕐 Tue–Sun 9–6 ✋ Moderate

🍴 Restaurants and cafés ($–$$) on the *zócalo*

GUADALAJARA

Mexico's second-largest city offers a compact historical center and lively traditions from *mariachis* to glass-blowing. The monuments are dotted around four central plazas surrounding the Catedral, a massive edifice that combines numerous architectural styles. Flanking the Plaza de Armas outside is the Palacio Nacional, where Miguel Hidalgo declared an end to slavery, an event captured by Orozco's powerful murals on its walls.

Immediately north is the **Museo Regional de Jalisco** (1701) housed in a former seminary. Exhibits cover pre-Hispanic artifacts, religious and colonial paintings, decorative arts and handicrafts by Jalisco's Huichol and Cora Indians. To the east stands the neo-classical Teatro Delgollado, where Guadalajara's state orchestra and Grupo Folklórico perform. From here, the Plaza Tapatía stretches east to the impressive Instituto Cultural Cabañas. This is the focal point for the city's cultural activities, as well as housing a homage to José Clemente Orozco, the city's renowned 20th-century painter, whose vigorous murals adorn the domed chapel.

Other offerings include a labyrinthine crafts and food market, the Mercado Libertad, and the Plaza de los Mariachis.

Don't miss Tlaquepaque and Tonalá, now engulfed by the urban sprawl. Tlaquepaque makes a colorful outing by bus from the center. Elegant 19th-century mansions converted into restaurants and crafts boutiques radiate from the Jardín Hidalgo and El Parián. Nearby lies Tonalá, with its glass and pottery workshops.

🚋 14J

ℹ️ Monumento Los Arcos, Avenida Vallarta 2641, Zona Minerva ☎ (333) 616 9150 🕐 Mon–Sat 9–7

Museo Regional de Jalisco

✉️ Corner Avenida Hidalgo and Liceo ☎ (33) 3614 9957 🕐 Tue–Sat 9–5:30, Sun 9–5 ✋ Moderate 🍴 Cafés and restaurants ($) on plazas

GUANAJUATO

Best places to see, pages 40–41.

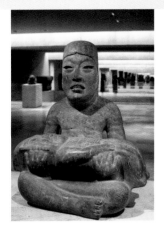

JALAPA (XALAPA)

Blazing sun in the morning and cooler mists in the afternoon characterize Jalapa's picturesque location, high in the coffee-growing hills inland from Veracruz. On the horizon is the Cofre de Perote volcano (4,282m/14,049ft) overlooking this lively university town, with its atmospheric colonial heart of steep, winding streets, gardens, parks and grandiose administrative buildings. The star sight is the excellent **Museo de Antropología,** an imaginatively designed modern building at the northern end of town. Here sunlit patios and terraced marble halls opening on to a landscaped park display a collection of the pre-Hispanic cultures of the Gulf region. Giant basalt heads from the Olmec center of San Lorenzo vie with the wonderful "smiling" sculptures of the Totonacs at El Tajín and the superb pottery of the northern Huastecs.

✚ 18J

🛈 Boulevard Cristóbal Colon 5

☎ (228) 812 8500

Museo de Antropología

✉ Avenida Xalapa, Estado de Veracruz

☎ (228) 815 0920 🕘 Tue–Sun 9–5

✋ Moderate 🍴 Cafeteria ($) in museum

LAGO DE CHAPALA

The warm climate of Mexico's largest natural lake has long attracted a stream of expatriates, from writers such as D. H. Lawrence and Sybille Bedford to today's 6,000 North American retirees. Sleepy fishing villages stud the lake shore, but the main action is along the northwest shore at Chapala, Ajijic and Jocotepec. Boat trips visit the two islands of Los Alacranes and Mexcala, the former boasting the lake's most scenic fish restaurants. More authentic in style, and the source of colorful handwoven *serapes* (shawls), is Jocotepec.

🚩 14J ✉ 50km (31 miles) southeast of Guadalajara, 40 mins by car 🍴 Vast choice of cafés and restaurants ($–$$$) along northwest shore

ℹ️ In Guadalajara (➤ 92)

MORELIA

The uncontested architectural jewel of fertile Michoacán is its capital, Morelia, a dynamic yet compact university town. Although founded in 1541 as Valladolid, it was renamed Morelia at independence to honor Jose María Morelos, a native son and key figure in the movement. Dominating the central plaza is a massive pink-stone cathedral, said to be the third largest in the Americas. Harmonious arcades, churches, colleges, and imposing colonial buildings radiate from here and include the magnificent mansion that now houses the **Museo Regional Michoacán,** covering local ethnography, archaeology, and colonial history. One block north is Mexico's oldest university, the Colegio de San Nicolás, and a few steps further the superbly proportioned Palacio Clavijero.

🚩 16J

ℹ️ Palacio Clavijero, Nigromante 79 ☎ (443) 312 8081

Museo Regional Michoacán

✉ Allende 305, corner of Abasolo ☎ (443) 312 0407

🕐 Tue–Sat 9–7, Sun 9–2. Closed Dec 25, Jan 1, Easter Sun 👆 Moderate 🍴 Cafés and restaurants ($) on square

PÁTZCUARO

Situated beside a tranquil lake, Pátzcuaro is an unusual and delightful little town. Quaint cobbled streets lined with neat whitewashed houses wind uphill from Plaza Vasco de Quiroga and Plaza Gertrudis Bocanegra to reach the Basílica de Nuestra Señora de la Salud. Founded in 1554 but rebuilt in 1883, the church contains a much revered corn-paste statue of the Virgin of Health, and on the eighth day of every month pilgrims flock here with requests. Close by is the **Museo de Artes Populares,** housed in a former college dating from 1540. Inside are displayed Michoacán's rich local crafts, from lacquerware to copper. Downhill from Plaza Gertrudis Bocanegra is the lake. From the main *embarcadero*, boats ferry visitors to the commercialized island of Janitzio. Crowning its hilltop is a gigantic statue of Morelos.

✚ 15J

ℹ Plaza Vasco de Quiroga 50, Guion A ☎ (434) 342 1214

Museo de Artes Populares

✉ Enseñanza y Alcantarilla ☎ (434) 342 1029 🕐 Tue–Sat 9–7, Sun 9–3 💰 Inexpensive 🍴 Cafés and restaurants ($) on main plazas

PUEBLA

Ringed by four volcanoes, including Popocatépetl and Iztacchíhuatl, and less than two hours by road from the capital is Puebla, Mexico's fourth-largest city. Though very industrialized, it is surprisingly easy-going, and offers fabulous examples of baroque architecture, in particular the Templo de Santo Domingo. At the heart of this church is the Capilla del Rosario (1690), the most sumptuous Dominican construction in the world, where gilded and carved stucco blankets the dome and walls as a backdrop to a bejeweled figure of the Virgin.

The 17th-century Ex-Convento de Santa Rosa, now converted into the Museo de las Artesanías, houses the nuns' kitchens where it is said the famed Pueblan *mole* sauce was invented. Religious art is exhibited at the Ex-Convento de Santa Monica, full of disguised doorways and secret passageways, dating from 1857 when President Juárez closed all religious structures.

Flanking the south of the *zócalo* is the vast Catedral, a mixture of various styles due to its prolonged construction between 1575 and 1649. Three blocks southeast is the impressively designed **Museo Amparo,** successfully incorporating high-tech displays of archaeology and viceregal art into a converted 16th-century hospital. Puebla is noted for the Talavera tiles that adorn many facades or domes. Particularly exceptional is the Casa de Alfeñique, home to the Museo Regional, while at Uriarte (➤ 110) workshops still make this renowned decorative ceramic.

🔳 17K

ℹ️ Avenida 5 Oriente (southern side of Catedral)

☎ (222) 246 2044/1285

Museo Amparo

✉ Calle 2 Sur, corner Avenida 9 Oriente ☎ (222) 229 3850 🕙 Wed–Mon 10–6 ✋ Moderate

🍴 Cafés and restaurants ($) on zócalo

a drive around Lake Pátzcuaro

Head out of Pátzcuaro on the road to the lake, then follow Highway 14 to Tzintzuntzán, about 20km (12 miles) away.

Above the town is Las Yacatas, a row of stepped, circular pyramids offering sweeping lake views and a small museum. In Tzintzuntzán itself stands the partly ruined 16th-century Templo de San Francisco. Close by are numerous craft outlets for local pottery, woodcarving, and straw figures.

Continue to Quiroga, the largest commercial town on the lake. Turn left at the main square for a short drive to Santa Fe de la Laguna.

It was here in the 1540s that Don Vasco de Quiroga, Michoacán's first bishop, attempted to set up a model

community based on Thomas More's *Utopia*. The 16th-century hospital and chapel still stand and the village square has been completely renovated, together offering an unusual stop.

Continue to skirt the lake through pine forests to the promontory of Chupicaro.

Next stop is San Jerónimo, a sprawling lakeside village jutting out on a small promontory, where activities concentrate on woodcarving and boatbuilding.

Drive on about 15km (9 miles) to the neighboring villages of Puacuaro, Napizaro, and Erongaricuaro.

The pure Purepecha inhabitants of Puacuaro and Napizaro specialize in basket-making. In Erongaricuaro (meaning "look-out tower on the lake") visit the 16th-century Franciscan church and seminary. Handicrafts made here include inlaid furniture, weaving, and embroidery.

The road continues around the lake through San Francisco Uricho, Arocutín, Tocuaro, and San Pedro, before rejoining Highway 14 and returning to Pátzcuaro.

Distance About 65km (40 miles)
Time Allow a leisurely day to include stops
Start/end point Pátzcuaro ✚ 15J
Lunch Restaurants ($) at Chupicaro

QUERÉTARO

The prosperous, industrial town of Querétaro has
a harder edge than its neighbors, yet despite this
it is rich in history, with a wealth of baroque
architecture and a monumental aqueduct (1735).
From the central church of San Francisco, a pedestrianized area,
dense with street stalls, leads uphill to the shady, porticoed Plaza
de las Armas. This focal point is the site of the 18th-century
Government Palace, situated beside several imposing mansions.

Adjoining San Francisco in another former convent is the
fabulous Museo Regional, with its renowned collection of
viceregal paintings. Southwest from here are Querétaro's two
baroque jewels, the Templo de Santa Clara (1633), with walls
covered in high-relief altarpieces, and the equally magnificent
Templo de Santa Rosa (1752). East of San Francisco stands the
church and former Convento de Santa Cruz (1654) that served as a
prison for Emperor Maximilian before his execution in 1867.

✚ 16J

ℹ Plaza de Armas ☎ (442) 238 5073

SAN MIGUEL DE ALLENDE

This small, picturesque town buzzes with U.S. expatriates,
students, and visitors. Reflecting this influx is a plethora of cafés,
bars, restaurants, and stores geared to their needs. Rising above
lively Plaza Allende are the lofty, neo-gothic spires of the Parroquía
(1880), while across a side street stands the 18th-century
birthplace of Ignacio Allende, an Independence protagonist. Now
the Museo Regional, it illustrates the city's history and archaeology
alongside contemporary art. Another impressive 18th-century
mansion is the Casa del Mayorazgo; its restored interior now
houses an art collection. This artistic theme continues in
exhibitions at the Centro Cultural Ignacio Ramírez.

✚ 16H

ℹ Plaza Allende ☎ (415) 152 6565

EL TAJÍN

Set in lush, scenic hills are the magnificent ruins of the Totonac civilization (4th–12th centuries). The nearest base is 12km (7 miles) away at the pretty little town of Papantla. El Tajín's main sight is the striking, tiered Pirámide de los Nichos (Pyramid of the Niches), incorporating 365 niches, rising beside numerous other buildings and at least 10 ball courts. The main ball-court walls are carved with fine bas-reliefs depicting players, sacrifices, and *pulque*-drinking. Uphill lies El Tajín Chico, where more structures surround the Edificio de las Columnas, decorated with intricate stone mosaics. At the entrance, outside the excellent modern museum, a 30m (100ft) pole is used by local *voladores* (flying dancers) to re-enact a dangerous but spectacular Totonac ritual.

✚ 18J ✉ Highway 130, Estado de Veracruz (25km/15 miles southeast of Poza Rica) ☎ (784) 842 0026 🕐 Daily 9–6 ✋ Moderate 🍴 Café ($) on site ❓ *Voladores* perform at noon daily

TAXCO

Best places to see, pages 50–51.

TEOTIHUACÁN

Best places to see, pages 52–53.

HOTELS

CUERNAVACA
♛♛♛♛ Las Mañanitas ($$$)

This restored hacienda is set in meticulously manicured grounds with extensive landscaping and a waterfall. The elegant rooms contain Spanish colonial furniture and painting by some of Mexico's finest artists, and the considerate, friendly staff will make you feel very welcome.

✉ Calle Ricardo Linares 107 ☎ (777) 314 1466; www.lasmananitas.com.mx

GUADALAJARA
♛♛ Hotel Frances ($$)

The popular, historic Hotel Frances, dating back to 1610, is just a few yards from Plaza de la Liberación and is full of Old World charm. Facilities include an inside patio, restaurant and bar. No two rooms are alike.

✉ Maestranza 35 ☎ (33) 3613 1190; www.hotelfrances.com

GUANAJUATO
♛♛ Hotel San Diego ($$)

The San Diego, overlooking the historic town's main square, offers reasonable rooms and a restaurant.

✉ Jardín de la Unión 1 ☎ (473) 732 1300

♛♛ Posada Santa Fé ($$$)

This elegant 19th-century mansion has antique furnishings and well-appointed rooms. It also boasts an excellent restaurant with outside tables on the main square. Parking is available.

✉ Jardin de la Union 12 ☎ (473) 732 0084

MEXICO CITY
♛♛ Best Western Hotel de Cortés ($$)

This legendary hotel occupies a former 18th-century hospice. In can be noisy, but it's in a good location and has a courtyard restaurant.

✉ Hidalgo 85, Centro ☎ (55) 5518 2181 🚇 Hidalgo

◈◈ Best Western Hotel Majestic ($$)

Plum location overlooking Zócalo. Colonial-style décor, terrace restaurant.

✉ Madero 73, Centro ☎ (55) 5521 8600 🚇 Zócalo

◈◈◈◈ Hotel Centro Historico ($$$)

This high-rise hotel is geared to businesspeople but there are some special rates worth looking for. The corner rooms have great panoramic views.

✉ Avenida Juárez 70, Centro ☎ (55) 5130 5300 🚇 Juárez, Bellas Artes

◈◈◈ La Casona ($$$)

Luxury boutique-style hotel, set in the heart of the city. Excellent service, beautiful furnishings.

✉ Durango 280 ☎ (55) 5286 3001 🚇 Sevilla

MORELIA

◈◈ Hotel de la Soledad ($$)

This small-scale hotel lies just north of the cathedral. The comfortable rooms are decorated with carved wood furniture and surround a peaceful, central courtyard with a fountain

✉ Zaragoza 90 y Melchor Oca ☎ (443) 312 1888

PUEBLA

◈◈◈◈ Camino Real Puebla ($$$)

The sumptuous Camino Real Puebla, a block from the *zócalo*, occupies the former Covento de la Concepción. Rooms are furnished with huge oak beds, antique wardrobes and colonial-era art.

✉ 7 Poniente 105, Centro Historico ☎ (222) 229 0909

QUERÉTARO

◈◈◈ Hotel Meson de Santa Rosa ($$$)

This restored 18th-century guest house stands on the main plaza. Rooms and spacious and comfortable, the decoration simple and tasteful; a few have private balconies

✉ Pasteur Sur 17 ☎ (442) 224 2623

SAN MIGUEL DE ALLENDE
💎💎 Hotel Posada de San Francisco ($$–$$$)
Excellent colonial-style hotel. Small but well-furnished rooms with
heating. Restaurant in front courtyard.
✉ Plaza Principal 2 ☎ (415) 152 7213

RESTAURANTS

GUADALAJARA
El Abajeño ($$)
A Guadalajaran landmark with top mariachis thrown in. Attractive
courtyard dining and bar, Jaliscan specialties and friendly service.
✉ Avenida Vallarta 2802, Minerva ☎ (33) 3630 0307 🕔 Lunch and dinner

💎💎💎 El Sacromonte ($$)
There's a casual atmosphere and excellent Nuevo Mexican cuisine
on offer in this neighbourhood restaurant, popular with locals and
visitors. Specialty dishes include *quesadillas cibeles* with rose
petals in a strawberry sauce.
✉ Pedro Moreno 1398 ☎ (33) 3823 5447 🕔 Lunch and dinner

GUANAJUATO
💎💎 El Gallo Pitagórico ($)
Enjoy the stunning view over central Guanajuato as you dine on
Mediterranean cuisine – salads, seafood, pasta (the lasagne is
particularly good) and meat with rich sauces.
✉ Constancia 10 ☎ (473) 732 9489 🕔 Lunch and dinner. Closed Mon

💎💎💎 Real de la Esperanza ($$)
This converted chapel is set high above the town offering
sweeping views, an outdoor bar area and sophisticated cuisine.
✉ Carretera Guanajuato-Dolores Hidalgo Km 5, Valenciana ☎ (473) 732
1041 🕔 From 1pm

MEXICO CITY
Cicero ($$)
Refined Mexican cuisine in a theatrical hacienda-style setting, with
antiques and a cosy wood-paneled bar. This is the place to indulge

to the full – try the plantains stuffed with ground beef as a starter.
Live music means a cover charge.

✉ londres 195, Zona Rosa ☎ (55) 5512 6868 🕐 Mon–Sat 1pm–1am
🚇 Sevilla

▽▽▽ Los Girasoles ($$)

Elegant setting overlooking Plaza Tolsa. Exquisite Mexican *nouvelle cuisine* inspired by pre-Hispanic recipes and ingredients. Try the turkey in tamarind *mole*. Good service, innovative *mariachis*, bar.

✉ Tacuba 8/10, Centro ☎ (55) 5510 0630 🕐 Sun–Mon 1–9pm, Tue–Sat 1pm–midnight 🚇 Bellas Artes

Hostería de Santo Domingo ($$)

Claims to be Mexico City's oldest restaurant. Graffiti liberally adorns the walls between old photos and pictures. The specialty is *chiles en nogada* all year round. Reasonable quality, erratic but friendly service.

✉ Belisario Domínguez 72, Centro ☎ (55) 5526 5276 🕐 Daily 10am–10:30pm 🚇 Allende

Madero ($)

Popular local restaurant buzzing with afternoon activity. Good-value set menus served 2–5pm. Useful stop-over location between Zócalo and Bellas Artes.

✉ Francisco Madero 36, Centro ☎ (55) 5510 2761 🕐 Lunch, dinner daily until 9:30 🚇 Allende

▽▽▽ ▽▽▽ Restaurant Antigua San Angel Inn ($$$)

The place to lunch or dine in elegant San Angel. A superb 18th-century hacienda with gardens and patio. Award-winning international cuisine. Booking is essential, but the patio also functions as a relaxing bar.

✉ Diego Rivera 50, corner Altavista, San Angel ☎ (55) 5616 2222
🕐 Mon–Sat 1pm–1am, Sun 1–10pm 🚇 Miguel Allende de Quevedo, then take taxi

Sanborns ($)

Spectacular atrium restaurant in the historic Casa de los Azulejos (House of Tiles). After your meal, take a look at Orozco's 1925 mural, "Omniscience" or do some shopping here.

✉ Francisco Madero 4, Centro ☎ (55) 5512 7824 🕑 Daily 7am–1am
🚇 San Juan de Letrán

MORELIA
☗☗☗ Fonda Las Mercedes ($$)

Dine inside or out at this stylish but traditional restaurant in a converted mansion. The international menu includes generous steaks and crepes filled with squash and cheese. The elegant colonial surroundings add luster to this local gem.

✉ León Guzman 47 ☎ (443) 312 6113 🕑 Mon–Sat 1pm–1am, Sun 1–6

QUERÉTARO
El Meson de Chico El Rota ($)

One of several terrace restaurants on the main square. Excellent Caesar salad and *nopalitos con queso*. Meat and seafood dishes.

✉ Pasteur Sur 16, Centro ☎ (442) 212 4295 🕑 Daily for breakfast, lunch, dinner

☗☗☗ Los Espejos ($$)

Romantic courtyard dining in the stunning 300-year-old mansion-style Meson de Santa Rosa hotel. Not to be missed, if only for a drink. Excellent, friendly service.

✉ Pasteur 17 Sur ☎ (442) 242 2623 🕑 Lunch and dinner

SAN MIGUEL DE ALLENDE
☗☗ La Bella Italia ($)

See page 59.

☗☗☗ Nirvana ($$)

Take a break from Mexican food and enjoy the modern fusion cooking with dishes such as Peking duck with blackberry sauce. The interior design combines water features with lots of foliage.

✉ Mesones 101 ☎ (415) 150 0067 🕑 Wed–Mon 8am–10:30pm

SHOPPING

ARTS AND ANTIQUES
Bazar Unicornio
Large courtyard with an unusual selection of antiques, hand-painted ex-votos, crosses in embossed silver, and other religious objects.

✉ Hernández Macías 80, San Miguel de Allende ☎ (415) 152 1306

Casa Poblana
Attractively renovated building in heart of Puebla's antique district, near the Sunday antiques market of Plazuela de los Sapos. Contemporary home objects (glass, ceramics, wood) beside unusual antiques.

✉ Calle 6 Sur 406, Puebla ☎ (222) 242 0848

Plaza San Angel
Mexico City's largest antiques center. Furniture, paintings, decorative arts, silver, bric-à-brac. Weekend market stalls bring the area alive; watch out for copies.

✉ Plaza del Angel, Londres 161 and Hamburgo 150, Zona Rosa, Mexico City
🕓 Daily 10–8; antiques market Sat–Sun 10–4 🚇 Insurgentes

CLOTHING AND ACCESSORIES
Hermes
Not cheap, but Hermes is legendary for its silk scarves and designer leather goods.

✉ Presidente Msaaryk 422A, between Calderón de la Barca and Edgar Allen Poe, Mexico City ☎ (55) 5282 2118 🚇 Polanco

El Sombrero
Handmade straw and leather hats. Special orders made at San Francisco 30.

✉ San Francisco 14, San Miguel de Allende ☎ (415) 152 3675

Zara

Stylish clothes usually in synthetic blends, made in Spain and sometimes reasonably priced. Bags, shoes and accessories too.

✉ Madero 50, corner Isabel La Católica, Centro Histórico, Mexico City
☎ (55) 5525 1516 🚇 Zócalo or Allende

HANDICRAFTS

Avalos Brothers

One hundred years of glass-blowing experience, and you can watch them at work next to the store. Prices are generally good.

✉ Carretones 5, Centro Historico, Mexico City ☎ (55) 5522 5311
🕐 Mon–Fri 10–5

Bazar Romero & Flores

Large store with wide choice of metal lamps in copper, brass or perforated tin. Wrought-iron candle-holders, hand-blown glass.

✉ Ancha de San Antonio 13, San Miguel de Allende ☎ (415) 152 7274

Casa de Artesanía

Reasonable variety of crafts from central Mexico in store close to the historic hacienda outside town.

✉ Ex-Hacienda San Gabriel de Barrera, Marfil, Guanajuato ☎ (473) 772 2408 🕐 Wed–Sun 10–5

Casa del Inquisidor

Historic house converted into labyrinthine arts, crafts, and home furnishings store.

✉ Cuadrante 36, San Miguel de Allende ☎ (415) 152 1325

Casa Queretana de Las Artesanías

Sells a wide range of local craftwork and interior decoration items. Lace, bed and table linen, pottery, wooden furniture.

✉ Andador Libertad 52, Centro, Querétaro ☎ (442) 214 1235 🕐 Daily

Casillas Artesanías

Good selection of handmade furnishings and handicrafts from the states of Michoacán, Guanajuato, Jalisco, Puebla, and Oaxaca.

✉ San Diego 805, Colonia Vista Hermosa, Cuernavaca ☎ (777) 316 3598
🕐 Daily

Cerámica Santa María
Demonstrates and sells handpainted pottery. Techniques and designs developed over 40 years.
✉ Zapata 900, Centro, Cuernavaca ☎ (777) 313 0670

Florería Encanto
Large store with good selection of reasonably priced pottery from Dolores Hidalgo and glassware from Guadalajara.
✉ Pasteur Sur 29, Querétaro ☎ (442) 212 3737

Fonart
Wide selection of Mexican handicrafts at this state-owned store. Fixed prices and top quality.
✉ Casa del Conde de la Valenciana, Km 5, Guanajuato ☎ (473) 772 2550
🕐 Daily 10–6

Fonart
Three branches of this state-run handicrafts store promise top-quality goods. You'll find excellent carved wooden furniture, pottery, ceramics, glass, textiles, jewelry, basket-ware, and more. Shipping arranged, fixed prices. The largest choice is at Patriotismo branch.
✉ Avenida Patriotismo 691, Mixcoac. Also at Avenida Juárez 89, Centro; Presidente Carranza 115, Coyoacán, Mexico City ☎ (55) 5563 4060
🕐 Mon–Sat 9–9, Sun 10–7 🚇 Mixcoac (main branch)

Fonart
Dependable state-owned handicrafts store with items from all over the country. Policy aims to give artisans better prices.
✉ Angela Peralta 20, Centro, Querétaro ☎ (442) 212 2648

Gezem
Colonial-style emporium, selling a range of handicrafts and silver.
✉ Benito Juarez 82, Taxco ☎ (762) 622 7539

La Luna Descalza
Good selection and imaginative display of handicrafts from all over Mexico. Lots of decorative tinwork. Near Bazar Sábado.
✉ Plaza San Jacinto 3, San Ángel, Mexico City ☎ (55) 5616 4617 🚌 San Ángel pesero bus down Insurgentes

Uriarte
Renowned workshop and outlet for traditional Talavera ceramics, founded in 1824. Exquisitely hand-painted pieces, but expensive. Short tours of workshops.
✉ Avenida 4 Poniente 911, between Calle 9 and 11, Puebla ☎ (222) 232 1598 🕐 Mon–Sat 10–6, Sun 11–6:30

JEWELRY
Bazar del Centro
Attractive jewelry emporium specializing in pearls and loose semi-precious and precious stones.
✉ Isabel la Católica 30, Centro Histórico, Mexico City ☎ (55) 5510 1840 🚇 Pino Suárez

La Bella Elena
Unusual silver and amber jewelry designs. Near the Sunday antiques market on Plazuela de los Sapos. Upstairs café-bar.
✉ Calle 6 Sur 310, Puebla ☎ (222) 242 0702

Lapidario Barrera
Designers Salvador Barrera and Lorena Chávez sell their beautifully made Mata Ortíz line of silver jewelry here
✉ Calle Juan Ruíz Alarcón 3, Taxco ☎ (762) 622 8707

Talleres de los Ballesteros
Jewelry, tableware and other decorative items in sterling silver.
✉ Amberes 24, Zona Rosa, Mexico City ☎ (55) 5511 8281 🚇 Insurgentes

MARKETS
Bazar Sábado
Upscale handicrafts bazaar in the southern San Ángel

neighborhood spills onto sidewalks (pavements). Few bargains in silver, ceramics, glass, clothing, and textiles, but a lively atmosphere.

✉ Plaza San Jacinto 11, San Ángel, Mexico City ⏰ Sat only 10–6 🚌 San Ángel pesero bus down Insurgentes

Casa de las Artesanías

A vast handicrafts emporium located in a former convent. Wide choice of Michoacán lacquerware, woodcarvings, pottery, copper and furniture. Small museum on premises. Shipping arranged. Market stalls in plaza outside.

✉ Ex-Convento de San Francisco, Plaza Valladolid, Morelia ☎ (443) 312 2486 ⏰ Daily 10–3, 5–8

La Ciudadela

An open-air treasure trove of handicrafts from all over the country surrounds a central courtyard. Bargaining is essential.

✉ Mercado de las Artesanías, Plaza de la Ciudadela, Calle Balderas, Mexico City ⏰ Mon–Sat 11–7, Sun 11–5 🚇 Juárez or Balderas

Mercado Hidalgo

Superb turn-of-the-20th-century iron-and-glass market building in the center with food market on the ground floor and upstairs stalls selling baskets, embroidered clothes, pottery, shawls and more.

✉ Avenida Juárez, Guanajuato ⏰ Daily 7am–9pm

Mercado La Victoria

Central market next to Santo Domingo church. Upper floor offers Pueblan food specialties and wide range of handicrafts from the region. Some upscale craft shops on ground level.

✉ Calle 5 de Mayo, between Avenida 8 and 6, Puebla ⏰ Mon–Sat 10:30–8

ENTERTAINMENT

NIGHTLIFE

Ballet Folklórico

Spellbinding panorama of Mexico's diverse traditional dance, music, and costumes from Aztec times to today's fiestas. The best opportunity to witness the country's rich performing arts in one fell swoop. Tickets through hotels or Ticketmaster.

✉ Palacio de Bellas Artes, Mexico City ☎ (55) 5512 2593/5521 3633
🕓 Wed and Sun 8:30pm, Sun 9:30am 🚇 Bellas Artes

Bar León

Large dance hall with live bands beating out tropical sounds till late. Gets very crowded. Fun, young crowd.

✉ Calle Brasil 5, Centro Histórico, Mexico City ☎ (55) 5510 3093
🕓 Mon–Sat 9pm–3am 🚇 Zócalo

Bar Mata

Bar on third and top-floor terrace of a historic building. An old favorite for late drinks.

✉ Filomena Mata 11, corner 5 de Mayo, Centro Histórico, Mexico City
☎ (55) 5518 0237 🕓 Tue–Sun 8pm–2am 🚇 Bellas Artes

SPORTS

Amigos del Río

White-water rafting at all levels in the lush tropical surroundings of the state of Veracruz.

✉ Calle Chilpancingo 205, Colonia Progreso, 91130 Jalapa ☎ (228) 815 8817

Expediciones México Verde

Experienced white water rafting agency with expeditions all over Mexico. River-rafting season coincides with rains (Jun–Oct).

✉ José Maria Vigil 2406, Colonia Italia Providencia, 44610 Guadalajara
☎ (33) 3641 5598

Fiesta Charra

Mexico's exciting rodeo. The *charread* features horsemanship and lassoing skills.

✉ Rancho del Charro, Avenida Constituyentes 500, Bosque de Chapultepec, Mexico City ☎ (55) 5277 8706 🕓 Sun noon 🚇 Constituyentes

The North and Baja California

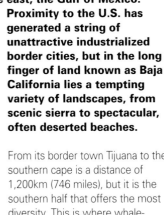

La Paz

Northern Mexico is the land of interminable desert rising abruptly into the Sierra Tarahumara and its canyons (► 36–37), while the coastlines are washed by the Pacific Ocean, the Mar de Cortés and, to the east, the Gulf of Mexico. Proximity to the U.S. has generated a string of unattractive industrialized border cities, but in the long finger of land known as Baja California lies a tempting variety of landscapes, from scenic sierra to spectacular, often deserted beaches.

From its border town Tijuana to the southern cape is a distance of 1,200km (746 miles), but it is the southern half that offers the most diversity. This is where whale-watching, bird-watching, sport fishing, scuba diving, riding, and trekking take over, backed up by still-fledgling coastal resorts that contrast with remote Jesuit missions in the sierra.

BAHÍA DE LOS ANGELES

This starkly beautiful bay on the Mar de Cortés makes a welcome change from the dry inland desert and is easily reached from the main highway, 68km (42 miles) away. Facilities include an airstrip, several good hotels, RV parks, restaurants, and the Museo Naturaleza y Cultura. On the horizon lies Isla Angel de la Guarda, a large island reserve, while the waters of the bay are alive with dolphins, finback whales, and sea lions. Boat trips can be arranged.

✚ 3C

BARRANCA DEL COBRE

Best places to see, pages 36–37.

CASAS GRANDES

This is the most important archaeological site in northern Mexico, best reached from Ciudad Juárez. Thought to date from AD1000, Casas Grandes (Paquimé) was abandoned in the mid-14th century following attacks by Apaches. Structures on site include platforms, ball courts, underground chambers, and the remains of three-story adobe houses. Excavations have unearthed rich finds of Paquimé pottery, necklaces of semi-precious stones, and carvings of Quetzalcóatl, some displayed in the museum.

✚ 6B ✉ Zona Arqueológica de Paquimé, Casas Grandes
☎ (636) 692 4140 🕐 Tue–Sun 10–5 💷 Moderate
🍴 Cafeteria ($)

CHIHUAHUA

Capital of Mexico's largest state, Chihuahua means "dry, sandy place" in Náhuatl, yet today this region prospers thanks to cattle ranches, silver, gold and copper mines, and apple orchards. The city is the eastern terminus for the Chihuahua–Pacífico railroad (➤ 36–37), but also offers a number of sights, some linked to Chihuahua's role in the War of Independence and the Revolution. On the central *zócalo* stands the baroque Catedral, and two blocks east is the Palacio Federal, where Miguel Hidalgo was imprisoned in 1811 before his execution. Opposite stands the pink Palacio del Gobierno, originally a Jesuit college, with murals depicting Chihuahua's history.

South of the center are two major museums. The Museo Regional is housed in the Quinta Gameros, a lavishly decorated mansion displaying art nouveau kitsch and a display of Paquimé pottery from Casas Grandes. Four blocks south is the **Museo de la Revolución,** in the mansion where revolutionary leader Pancho Villa lived. Exhibits include photographs, arms, documents, and the black 1922 Dodge peppered with bullet holes in which Villa was assassinated.

➕ 7C

🛈 Palacio de Gobierno, Plata Baja, Centro ☎ (614) 410 1077

Museo de la Revolución

✉ Calle Décima 3014 ☎ (614) 416 2958 🕐 Tue–Sat 9–1, 3–7, Sun 10–4 Inexpensive

ENSENADA

Just over 100km (62 miles) south of
Tijuana lies Ensenada, Baja California's
most popular resort, receiving half a million
visitors each year. These are mostly
Californians on weekend drinking, eating,
shopping, and sport fishing sprees, but
during the week the town and its bay
return to more tranquil fishing and shipping
activities. Ultra-fresh seafood is available at
the Mercado de Pescas opposite the pier,
and local wine can be sampled at the
wineries. The largest, **Bodegas Santo
Tomás,** offers daily wine tastings in its
converted warehouse.

South of town is La Bufadora, a blowhole where wave action
produces a dramatic geyser, and the secluded beach of Punta
Banda. Nearby are the surfers' favorites of San Miguel, Tres
Marías, California, and La Joya.

➕ 1A

ℹ️ Tourist and Convention Bureau, Lázaro Cárdenas, corner Miramar

☎ (646) 172 3022

Bodegas Santo Tomás

✉ Avenida Miramar 666 ☎ (646) 178 3333 🕐 Daily tours at 11, 1, 3

✋ Moderate

GUERRERO NEGRO

Although ostensibly a dull town of endless saltflats, vats, and
warehouses, Guerrero Negro is also the entry point to the Laguna
Ojo de Liebre (Scammon's Lagoon), a protected national park
where gray whales come to breed between December and March.
Lookout posts dot the shore and skiffs can be rented at the beach.

➕ 2C ❓ Reserva de la Biosfera El Vizcaino ☎ (615) 157 1777/0177;
Eco-Tours Malarrimo ☎ (615) 157 0100

HERMOSILLO

The industrialized city of Hermosillo appears to have little charm, yet its strategic site, 225km (140 miles) south of the border town of Nogales on Highway 15, with access to the beach resorts of Guaymas and Bahía Kino, about 100km (62 miles) west, makes it a good stop-over. The attractive colonial heart centers around the shady Plaza de Zaragoza, flanked by the Catedral and the Palacio de Gobierno. South of here lies the Centro Ecológico de Sonora, a zoo and botanical garden full of indigenous and desert specimens.

On the slopes of the Cerro de la Campaña, a hill overlooking the town, is the **Museo Regional de Sonora** in a converted penitentiary and, further north, the Ciudad Universitario, with its museum of local silk production.

✚ 4C

ℹ Palacio de Gobierno, Edificio Norte, Paseo Río Sonora

☎ (662) 172 964

Museo Regional de Sonora

✉ Jesús García Finál, corner Estéban Sarmiento ☎ (662) 217 1241 🕐 Tue–Sat 10–5:30, Sun 9–4 💰 Moderate; free Sun

LA PAZ

The prosperous capital of Baja California Sur (south Baja), La Paz, lies on a large bay opening on to the Mar de Cortés, an ecologically rich gulf dotted with island nature reserves. Protected to the north by the peninsula of El Mogote, whose shores teem with resort hotels, downtown La Paz looks directly west across the bay. This provides a major natural feature – dramatic sunsets.

La Paz (ironically meaning "peace") suffered a turbulent past, set in motion by Hernán Cortés in 1535. Vicious conflicts with the indigenous inhabitants were exacerbated over the centuries by droughts, famines, smallpox, pirates, American troops during the Texan War and, in 1853, the infamous William Walker, intent on installing slavery. As a result, no indigenous groups survived in Baja. The town's fortunes were revived partly thanks to American sport fishermen, ferry services, the Transpeninsular highway and its free-port status, so that today La Paz boasts one of Mexico's highest per-capita incomes.

The center of La Paz radiates from Plaza Constitución, where the Palacio de Gobierno faces the picturesque 19th-century Catedral de la Señora de la Paz, built on the site of a 1720 mission. Close by is the Teatro de la Ciudad, where modern facilities include art galleries and a library. La Paz's history is covered at the **Museo de Antropología,** where informative displays illustrate Baja geology, the early Pericu, Cochimi and Guaicura inhabitants and information on the cave paintings near San Ignacio (➤ 125).

The balmy climate, averaging 25°C (77°F), constant breezes and scenic palm-fringed *malecón* (seafront promenade) make La Paz a relaxing base for exploring the inland sierra, indulging in endless watersports or boat trips, or enjoying the fine white sand of its

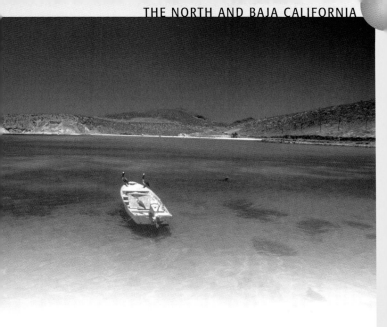

beaches. The modernized town center has few historical sights, but Baja is, after all, about the great outdoors.

Although the primary winter (January–March) grounds for humpback whales are around Los Cabos, they sometimes venture into the Bay of La Paz.

Year-round boat trips go to Isla Partida, a seal sanctuary, and the islands of Cerralvo and Espíritu Santo, both nature reserves that offer diving and swimming in the transparent waters of their coves. Sport fishing meanwhile takes advantage of the 850 species of fish in the warm waters of the gulf.

➕ 4F

ℹ️ Carretera al Norte Km 5.5 ☎️ (612) 124 0100. Small office on Tourist Wharf, Paseo Alvaro Obregón 2130 🕐 Mon–Sat

Museo de Antropología

✉️ Calle Altamirano, corner 5 de Mayo ☎️ (612) 122 0162 🕐 Mon–Fri 8–6, Sat 9–2 💰 Free 🍽️ Cafés and restaurants ($) on Plaza Constitución

a drive through Southern Baja

This drive circles the southern tip of Baja California, passing through dramatic sierra and tiny villages, with a night stop at Los Cabos.

From La Paz drive south on Highway 1 before taking the left fork at San Pedro. From here the road winds up to El Triunfo.

Rich silver veins were discovered here in 1862, leading to a population explosion till the mines closed down in 1926. The town is now virtually a ghost town though small-scale mining has resumed.

Continue 8km (5 miles) to San Antonio, a farming and former silver-mining town, before twisting up into the Sierra El Triunfo. The road descends again to the coast at Los Barriles, renowned for its spectacular winds.

Stop here for a refreshing swim in the Bahía de las Palmas before lunch.

The road skirts the coast before twisting inland and climbing past small villages. About 4km (2.5 miles) beyond Santiago it crosses the Tropic of Cancer, marked by a concrete sphere. At Las Casitas, the road widens to descend to San José del Cabo (➤ 122–123), an ideal overnight stop. Next morning, head for Cabo San Lucas along the coastal highway and drive to the marina.

Stop here for a glass-bottomed boat trip around the striking rock formation known as El Arco (The Arch).

Drive out of town on Highway 9 to Todos Santos, 80km (50 miles) to the north.

This quiet farming town is attracting a growing community of Americans and a small arts and crafts industry. Beautiful Playa Punta Lobos and Playa San Pedrito are east of town. From here, 80km (50 miles) brings you back to La Paz.

Distance 397km (247 miles)
Time 2 days
Start/end point La Paz ✠ 4F
Lunch Hotel Palmas de Cortés ($$) ✉ Conocido en Los Barriles
☎ (624) 141 0050

LORETO

Loreto is a peaceful getaway in a beautiful setting, backed by the Sierra de la Giganta. The modest town center claims the well-preserved Jesuit mission, from where Father Junípero Serra set out in 1769 to establish a chain of 17 Californian missions. Inside, the **Museo de los Misiones** gives an informative introduction to local missionary activities. Around the church is a pedestrian area leading down to the harbor and beach where Loreto's few hotels are located. Activities include tennis at one of the world's most modern tennis centers, sport fishing, hiking, and scuba diving, as well as boat trips to the lovely Isla Coronado. A mega-resort planned 20km (12 miles) south at Puerto Loreto has been slow to develop.

✚ 4D

Museo de los Misiones

✉ Salvatierra 16 ☎ (613) 135 0005 🕐 Tue–Sun 9–1, 3–6 ✋ Inexpensive

🍴 Cafés ($) in nearby plaza

LOS CABOS

At the tip of Baja lie the twin resorts of Cabo San Lucas and San José del Cabo, 30 minutes apart but with quite distinct atmospheres. Cabo San Lucas is a boisterous, expensive, modern golf resort while San José retains a quaint Mexican village atmosphere beneath its touristic veneer. Los Cabos offer luxury hotels, golf courses, sport fishing, surfing, scuba diving at the unique underwater sand cascades, whale-watching, and horse riding in the sierra.

San José dates back to 1730 when its Jesuit mission was founded. Adjacent Paseo Mijáres, with its stone and stucco 19th-century houses, is now the focal point for restaurants, bars, stores and real-estate agents. At the river estuary, a small **Centro Cultural de Los Cabos** (cultural center) displays arts and crafts, fossils, and reproduction cave-paintings, while next to this is an ecological reserve, home to 200 bird species.

The Baja peninsula ends at El Arco, a massive rock arch that terminates the headland. Boat trips from the marina visit this landmark and El Faro Viejo (Old Lighthouse), which offers panoramic views. Pelicans, seals, sea lions, dolphins, and whales can be seen, while underwater is a paradise for snorkelers and divers.

www.visitloscabos.org

✚ 5F

🛈 Hwy 1, Plaza San José, San José del Cabo ☎ (624) 146 9628

Centro Cultural de Los Cabos

✉ Behind Presidente Forum Resort ☎ (866) LOSCABOS 🕔 Tue–Sun 9–5, Wed 9–1 ✋ Inexpensive 🍴 Cafés and restaurants ($$) on Paseo Mijáres

MULEGÉ

The sleepy oasis town of Mulegé overlooks the mouth of the 40km (25 miles) Bahía de Concepción, backed by the Sierra de Santa Lucía. The original settlement was founded beside Baja's only navigable river, whose water has nourished large groves of olive trees and date palms. On the hilltop above stands the 1705 Misión de Santa Rosalía, once an open prison and now the Museo de Mulegé, with an eclectic range of exhibits including old diving and mining equipment. Low-key Mulegé mainly attracts sport fishermen, but also offers kayaking upriver or to outlying islands, scuba diving, and jeep or horse-back trips to see the Cuevas de San Borjita paintings.

➕ 4D ✋ Moderate ❓ Kayaking and cave-painting tours through Hotel Hacienda, Calle Romero Rubio, Mulegé ☎ (800) 346 3942

SAN FELIPE

Running from the border town of Mexicali, Highway 5 ends at San Felipe, a fishing village that has become a resort. The main reason to come here is for the fishing. San Felipe also attracts beach-lovers, as its golden sands border the warm Mar de Cortés (as opposed to the chillier and rougher Pacific). Impressive tides make the beach south of town popular for dune-buggying, and this is where an increasing number of upscale hotels are appearing.

✠ 2A

🛈 Mar de Cortés corner Manzanillo ☎ (686) 577 1155

🕔 Tue–Sun 9–2, 4–6

SAN IGNACIO

This attractive oasis town on the edge of the Desierto de Vizcaíno makes a tranquil stop-over as well as being the entry point to Laguna San Ignacio, a major whale-watching spot 70km (43 miles) away. The little town itself features a shady plaza, a beautifully preserved mission church (1786), a small **museum** and date-palm groves planted by the Jesuits. Trips can be arranged to the lagoon during the whale season and all year into the nearby Sierra de San Francisco to see some of the 500 caves painted by the original inhabitants of the area centuries ago (reached by 4WD or horse- or mule-back only).

✠ 3D

Museo Pinturas Rupestres

✉ Misión de San Ignacio

☎ (615) 154 0222

🕔 Mon–Fri 8–3 💰 Moderate

HOTELS

CHIHUAHUA

▼▼▼ Best Western Mirador Motor Inn ($$)

This large, modern motel-style hotel is a short walk from the historic heart of the city and the shopping district. Rooms are clean and spacious, if basic.

✉ Avenida Universidad 1309 ☎ (614) 432 2200

▼ Hotel Divisadero Barrancas ($–$$)

Spectacularly situated, looking over Urique canyon. Good rooms, restaurant, bar, parking.

✉ Divisadero station, Urique ☎ (635) 415 1199

▼▼▼ Quality Inn San Francisco ($$)

Modern hotel behind the cathedral. Amenities include bar, restaurant, travel desk.

✉ Victoria 409 ☎ (614) 439 9000

CREEL

▼▼ Best Western The Lodge at Creel ($$)

The timber-clab cabins are exceptionally cosy, with blanket-laden beds and gas fireplaces. The large bar is the best bet in Creel if Tico Molcas is full.

✉ Avenida Lopez Mateos 61 ☎ (635) 456 0071

ENSENADA

▼ Best Western El Cid Hotel ($$)

Small-scale, Best Western hotel close to the bay. Strong accent on Mexican décor. Restaurant, bar, pool, parking.

✉ Avenida López Mateos 993 ☎ (646) 178 2401

LA PAZ

▼▼ Club El Moro ($)

Pleasant, friendly hotel across road from sea; air-conditioned rooms with satellite TV and balconies surrounding small pool.

✉ Km 2 Carretera Pichilingue, Colonia Colina del Sol ☎ (612) 122 4084

☜☜ Hotel Seven Crown ($$)

This oceanfront hotel is great for families, with large, brightly decorated rooms with twin beds. The restaurant on the fourth floor has spectacular views of the bay.

✉ Paseo Alvaro Obregon y Lerdo de Tejeda ☎ (612) 128 7787

LORETO

☜ Hotel La Pinta ($$$)

The small-scale Hotel La Pinta, in a beautiful setting right on the seafront, has good standard air-conditioned rooms complete with satellite TV. Attractive pool with *palapas* and sea view; restaurant, bar, parking. It makes an ideal base for fishing enthusiasts.

✉ Calle Francisco Madero, Playa Loreto ☎ (613) 135 0025

LOS CABOS

☜☜☜ Casa del Mar Beach Golf & Spa Resort ($$$)

Somewhat remote, this will appeal to people seeking seclusion. All the rooms have flatscreen televisions and Jacuzzis and the bedding and toiletries are of the highest standard. Guests can practise their golf swing at the Cabo Real course or relax in the Sueños del Mar spa.

✉ Carretera Transpeninsular KM19.5, San José del Cabo ☎ (624) 145 7700

☜☜☜ Casa Natalia ($$)

A well-established favorite of seasoned Los Cabos visitors, Casa Natalia is comfortable and charming, with an outstanding restaurant, Mi Cocina. San Jose's nightlife is also on your doorstep.

✉ Boulevard Mijares 4, San José del Cabo ☎ (624) 146 7100

☜☜ ☜☜ Esperanza Resort ($$$+)

Perhaps the most dramatic view of Cabo's famed landmark El Arco is from Esperanza, a plush, luxurious collection of 50 suites and six villas. Located at exclusive and exceptional Punta Ballena.

✉ Carretera Transpeninsular Km 7, Cabo San Lucas ☎ (624) 145 6400

RESTAURANTS

CHIHUAHUA
Chihuahua Charlie's ($)
A popular branch of the Anderson's chain of restaurants serving a wide choice of meat dishes and salads. Cheerful service and setting.
✉ Avenida Juárez 3329 ☎ (614) 415 7065

ENSENADA
🍷🍷🍷 **El Rey Sol ($$$)**
Award-winning restaurant serving French Provençal and Mexican dishes. Elegant, colonial-style setting.
✉ Avenida López Mateos 1000 ☎ (646) 178 1733 🕐 Lunch and dinner

GUERRERO NEGRO
Malarrimo ($–$$)
Delicious seafood including abalone, shrimp, and fish. Ask here about natural history and cave painting tours.
✉ Boulevard Emiliano Zapata (near entrance to town) ☎ (615) 157 0250

LA PAZ
Café Gourmet ($)
Beachfront restaurant on road towards Pichilingue peninsula. Wide selection, including seafood, salads.
✉ 2.5 Km Carretera Pichilingue ☎ (612) 125 2828 🕐 Tue–Sat 8am–10pm

🍷🍷 **Terraza del Perla ($)**
Open-air restaurant of an established seafront hotel. Popular for large breakfasts and great snacks at any time.
✉ Alvaro Obregón 1570 ☎ (612) 122 0777

LORETO
Café Olé ($)
Popular U.S.-style restaurant. Steaks, salads, and seafood; cheerful atmosphere.
✉ Madero 14 ☎ (613) 135 0495

Caesar's ($$)
See page 58.

LOS CABOS
✦✦ Damiana ($$)

Colorful, romantic restaurant with patio dining at the heart of San José. Sophisticated cuisine includes char-broiled lobster and jumbo prawns.

✉ Paseo Mijares 8, San José del Cabo ☎ (624) 142 0499 🕐 Daily 10:30–10:30 ❓ Reservation recommended

Edith's ($$$)

Mexican musicians give atmosphere to this classy small café where the home-made tortillas are the best for miles around and the desserts are a real treat,

✉ Paseo del Pescador, Cabo San Lucas ☎ (624) 143 0801 🕐 1–11pm

✦✦ Mama Mia ($)

Popular, relaxed restaurant. International dishes, seafood, live music, fun atmosphere.

✉ Km 29.5 Carretera Transpeninsular, San José del Cabo ☎ (624) 142 3940 🕐 Breakfast, lunch, and dinner

✦✦ Panchos ($$)

Colorful Mexican restaurant offering hearty traditional dishes and seafood. Tortilla soup, *chile relleno* and lobster specialties. Live music nightly.

✉ Calle Hidalgo, corner Zapata, Cabo San Lucas ☎ (624) 143 2891 🕐 6am–11pm

SHOPPING
CLOTHING AND ACCESSORIES
La Sandia

Stylish women's clothes, accessories and jewelry inspired by pre-Hispanic designs.

✉ Plaza Míjares 6-B, San José del Cabo ☎ (624) 142 2230

HANDICRAFTS
Casa Mexicana
Wide selection of Mexican handicrafts from Talavera pottery to wooden furniture.

☒ Main plaza, Avenida Cabo San Lucas, Cabo San Lucas ☎ (624) 143 1933
🕑 Daily 4–10pm

Copal
Attractively converted old house with fine selection of handicrafts from all over Mexico. Taxco silver, hand-blown glass, rattan furniture, masks, rugs, pottery.

☒ Plaza Mijares 10, San José del Cabo ☎ (624) 142 3070

ENTERTAINMENT

NIGHTLIFE
El Squid Roe
Without doubt, the craziest restaurant and dance club in Cabo. The place for frenzied dancing all night long.

☒ Larazo Cardenas at Boulevard, Cabo San Lucas ☎ Marina (624) 143 1269
🕑 12pm–3am or later

Tropicana Bar and Grill
Definitely a happening place to enjoy live music. The balcony overlooking the stage is the best spot to have a look before you hit the dance floor.

☒ Boulevard Mijares 30, San José del Cabo ☎ (624) 142 1580 🕑 2pm–3am

SPORTS

Cabo Aquadeportes
Scuba diving, equipment rental, instructors.

☒ Hacienda Hotel and Playa Chilena, Cabo San Lucas ☎ (624) 143 0017 or (800) 733 2226

Solmar Fleet
Sport fishing fleet with professional crews and all fishing equipment. For three to ten people.

☒ Solmar Hotel Desk, Cabo San Lucas ☎ (624) 143 0646/(800) 344 3349

Pacific Mexico

Mexico's oldest beach playgrounds are located along the Pacific coastline between Mazatlán and Acapulco. This is where the country's most dramatic beaches are found, backed by the craggy outline of the Sierra Madre del Sur. Glitzy favorites such as Acapulco and Puerto Vallarta are now joined by Ixtapa-Zihuatanejo, a burgeoning twin resort, and quieter destinations such as San Blas and Barra de Navidad, which offer a more genuine Mexican atmosphere.

Acapulco
de Juárez

Long tracts of coastline remain undeveloped, while short forays can be made inland to hill villages where church bells are the only interruption to a peaceful existence. Watersports are king in these deep blue waters that are sometimes unsuitable for swimming due to their treacherous currents. Acapulco and Puerto Vallarta are the places to go for nightlife, good restaurants, and shopping.

ACAPULCO

A stunning sweep of bay heralded Acapulco's rise to fame in the 1950s, a revival of its 16th-century fortunes when it was developed by Cortés and his men as a port. In 1565 the first galleon set sail from Manila in the Philippines (then under Spanish rule) to Acapulco, marking the beginning of a flourishing trade route that saw the wealth of the Orient exchanged with that of Nueva España.

With an international airport and a fast toll road from Mexico City, Acapulco's fortunes are assured. Lining its 11km (7-mile) horseshoe bay are endless high-rise hotels, nightclubs, restaurants, and a string of beaches where watersports and sun-worshipping set the tone. A concrete jungle or a steamy, sybaritic holiday playground? Opinions are divided, but every visitor is at least won over by the stunning scenery.

From the eastern headland of Playa Bruja, the Costera Miguel Alemán sweeps past a succession of facilities that include five golf courses, children's recreation parks, a crafts market and the San Diego Fort high above the old town, before the bay twists into a peninsula. To the west is the towering cliff of La Quebrada, where daredevil divers plunge into the waves, and beyond this the tranquil beach and Coyuca Lagoon at Pie de la Cuesta. Air-conditioned buses shuttle along the front, making travel easy. Family holidays are much helped by this excellent infrastructure, but remember that Acapulco is an oasis in one of Mexico's poorest states.

✠ 16L

🛈 Playa Los Hornos, Costera Miguel Alemán ☎ (74) 844583

Fuerte de San Diego

Overlooking the lively, narrow streets of the old town is this striking stone fort, with panoramic views over the bay and mountains. It was completed in 1617 to protect the thriving port from pirate and buccaneer attacks (including England's notorious Sir Francis Drake). Today, it functions as the Museo Histórico, with interesting historical and ethnographic exhibits.

✉ Calle Morelos and Playa Hornitos ☎ (744) 484 4583
🕐 Tue–Sun 9:30–6:30

Isla la Roqueta

A few hundred yards off the Peninsula de las Playas, this small island, reached by glass-bottomed boats from below the Fuerte de San Diego, offers relaxing respite from the main Costera. Cross the island to reach a small, secluded bay with a restaurant, or climb to the lighthouse. The waters are targeted by scuba divers, who come to see the underwater shrine of La Virgen Sumergida.
✉ Off Peninsula de las Playas

Pie de la Cuesta

This long, narrow spit of land separating the Pacific from the mangrove and palm-fringed Laguna Coyuca is a favorite with waterskiers. Sunset fanatics home in on the beach to watch the painted sky from a beach bar hammock and sponsor daredevil locals to pit their strength against the thundering surf. Sadly, in 1997 Hurricane Pauline did extensive damage to this stretch and it will be some time before it regains its idyllic backdrop.

✉ 11km (7 miles) northwest of Acapulco

La Quebrada

Acapulco's high divers plunge over 40m (130ft) from this cliff into the crashing surf of a narrow cove below. This sight is even more spectacular after sundown, when the last divers carry lighted torches as they plunge. Have dinner or a drink while you witness this carefully timed feat of bravura.

✉ Hotel Plaza Las Glorias, La Mira
🕐 Daily at 1, 7:15, 8:15, 9:15, 10:15pm 🖐 Inexpensive

More to see in Pacific Mexico

BARRA DE NAVIDAD

This picturesque fishing village developed into an alternative beach resort to soulless Manzanillo, about 60km (37 miles) south. Built on a sandbar next to a large estuary, Barra town offers modest hotels and restaurants, and safe swimming in a scenic setting. Towering above the town is the Grand Bay Hotel, Isla Navidad, with a 27-hole golf course, beach club and a glitzy marina.

✛ 13J ✉ 60km (37 miles) north of Manzanillo

ℹ Jalisco 67 ☎ (315) 355 5100

IXTAPA-ZIHUATANEJO

These twin resort towns are only 6km (4 miles) apart, yet have very different characters. Ixtapa is the modern half, its beachfront lined with high-rise hotels squeezed along the long white-sand Playa del Palmar. The wide bay dotted with tiny islands offers boat trips, windsurfing, waterskiing and diving, but swimming can be dangerous. When the waves are strong, head for Isla Ixtapa, where a secluded beach fronts a nature reserve. Ixtapa also offers excursions to lagoons, horse riding, sport fishing, golf, and diving.

For some, the former fishing-village setting of Zihuatanejo, with forested headlands plunging into secluded bays, is preferable. Although it is a jazzed-up version of its former self, it offers more atmosphere and older, less pretentious hotels. The least attractive beach, Playa Principal, edges the old town, but beyond a headland

to the southeast are Playa Madera, a family beach with economical hotels; Playa la Ropa, home to chic hotels; and Playa Las Gatas, only accessible by boat.

✛ 15K ⛴ Motorboats run all day from Playa Quieta, Ixtapa's northern beach, or sail there with Yates del Sol from Puerto Mío marina

ℹ Ixtapa shopping mall ☎ (755) 553 1967

MAZATLÁN

This sprawling resort town is also the largest west coast port between Los Angeles and the Panama Canal, a factor that makes it less commercialized than Mexico's other resorts. Jutting out on a peninsula marked by three hills, its beaches stretch for about 8km (5 miles), lined by a sea-wall promenade, the *malecón*, which ends at El Faro, the headland lighthouse. Behind this hilltop lies the commercial port and old town, while to the far north, Mazatlán's Zona Hotelera monopolizes the seafront.

Despite the influx of tourism, initially attracted by rich sport fishing, Mazatlán still depends on its fishing industry, with tuna-canning factories and shrimp-freezing plants supplied daily by Mexico's largest shrimp fleet. Fish aside, it offers great sports (golf, tennis, riding, watersports), boat trips to two islands with pristine beaches and an atmospheric old town center with a gracious old theater, cathedral, and a small archaeological museum, which displays locally excavated artifacts.

➕ 7F

ℹ️ Edificio Banrural, Avenida Camarón Sábalo

☎ (669) 916 5160

PUERTO VALLARTA

Puerto Vallarta is located on Mexico's largest bay, the Bahía de Banderas. It acquired international fame in 1964 when John Huston's film *The Night of the Iguana* hit the screens, with a hot background romance between Richard Burton and Elizabeth Taylor. At that time Vallarta was just a quaint little fishing village with cobbled streets and tile-roofed houses. Today this aspect still exists

(➤ 138–139), as does a moody backdrop of thickly forested hills that sometimes plunge straight into the Pacific, but beyond are high-rise hotels and condos, a marina, hip nightclubs, cosmopolitan restaurants and a vast array of high-quality stores.

Developments are spreading fast at both ends of the bay, to Mismaloya in the south, where an underwater park lies around the outlying rocks of Los Arcos, and 18km (11 miles) north to the self-contained Nueva Vallarta. Boat trips spirit you to beauty spots such as Boca de Tomatlán, Yelapa, or the Islas Marietas, off Punta Mita. Equally scenic are the roads through the hills, such as to El Tuito; horseback riding or biking are a good alternative to jeeps.

Old Vallarta is still unsurpassed for atmosphere; don't miss the *malecón* and Río Cuale environs. An island at the mouth of this river is home to the **Museo del Cuale,** restaurants, and craft shops, while on its north bank is the *malecón*, town hall and church. The backstreets here are packed with intriguing stores and art galleries. The liveliest town beach, day and night, is Playa Los Muertos, at the southern end of the town center.

✚ 13J

ℹ Local 18, Zona Comercial, Hotel Canto del Sol ☎ (322) 224 1175

Museo del Cuale

✉ Isla Cuale 🕔 Tue–Sat 10–3, 4–7, Sun 10–2

SAN BLAS

If you have a good insect repellent and revel in sleepy, unspoiled seaside towns, then this is where to go. Surfing is the number one activity here, closely followed by bird-watching in the mangrove-fringed estuaries and La Tovara lagoon. From November to March over 200 migrating species join the 150 native species. The bay was an important 16th- to 18th-century departure point for Spanish expeditions, and ruins from this period include the old Aduana (Customs House), the hilltop Fuerte de Basilio, and a 1769 church.

✚ 13H ✉ 130km (81 miles) northwest of Puerto Vallarta

ℹ Palacio Municipal ☎ (323) 285 0005

a walk in Puerto Vallarta

This walk winds through atmospheric cobbled streets and leads you across the Río Cuale (➤ 137) to where the Mexican heart still beats.

Start at the church on the main square of Old Vallarta.

The curious crown that tops Nuestra Señora de Guadalupe is a replica of the hapless Empress Carlota's crown. It fell off in a 1994 earthquake, but is now perfectly restored.

Leave the church, turn right into Hidalgo and right again up Iturbide. Climb two steep blocks to Carranza and turn right.

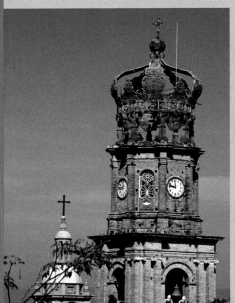

At the end of this street on the left is the Callejón de los Tarques, crossed by the bridge that Elizabeth Taylor and Richard Burton built to connect their two houses. There is a lovely view south from the corner.

Return along Carranza as far as Corona. Turn left and walk two blocks downhill for another superb view, looking north. Walk along Matamoros for five blocks, then turn left at Libertad. This goes over the Río Cuale into Insurgentes. Turn left at Lázaro Cárdenas.

On your left is Santa Cruz (built 1902), a popular neighborhood church.

Continue three blocks further to the Emiliano Zapata market on your right before turning left down Camichín. Climb a few steps at the end to a riverside road. Follow it into Aquiles Serdán and walk straight on, crossing Insurgentes, to Ignacio Vallarta, then turn right. This brings you to steps down on to the Isla Cuale below. Walk west towards the sea.

On your right is the small Museo del Cuale, with an interesting collection of pottery, sculptures and other artifacts from Jalisco, Narayit, and Colima.

Distance 3km (2 miles)
Time 2 hours
Start point Nuestra Señora de Guadalupe, Old Vallarta
End point Isla Cuale
Lunch Daiquri Dick's Restaurant/Bar ($–$$) ✉ Olas Altas 314
☎ (322) 222 0566
Museo del Cuale
✉ Isla Cuale ⏰ Tue–Sat 10–3, 4–7, Sun 10–2

HOTELS

ACAPULCO

❤❤❤❤ Camino Real Acapulco Diamante ($$$)

A full-service, luxury hotel. All rooms have scenic views of Puerto Marqués Bay and there's a selection of restaurants to choose from.

✉ Carretera Escénica Km 14 ☎ (744) 435 1010

❤❤❤ Hotel Elcano Royal ($$$)

Opposite golf course at eastern end of Costera, with pool over-looking beach. Spacious rooms, excellent restaurant, bars, good service.

✉ Avenida Costera Miguel Alemán 75 ☎ (744) 435 1500

❤❤❤ Hotel Las Brisas ($$$)

Located on a mountainside in a residential are, with excellent views. Popular with honeymooners.

✉ Carretera Escénica 5255 ☎ (744) 469 6900

IXTAPA-ZIHUATANEJO

❤❤ Best Western Hotel Posada Real ($$)

Good family-style seafront hotel with air-conditioned rooms, pool, children's playground, tennis, restaurant, bar, boat tours.

✉ Boulevard Ixtapa, Ixtapa ☎ (755) 553 0831

❤❤❤ Hotel Pacifico Dorada ($$$)

Spectacularly designed hotel, set in landscaped gardens, with a good beach location. The comfortable rooms have ocean views.

✉ Paseo de Ixtapa sin Lote 3-A ☎ (755) 553 2025

❤❤❤❤ La Casa Que Canta ($$$)

Set on a cliff with bay views. Facilities include a whirlpool and Well Being Center. Only a few rooms have elevator access.

✉ Camino Escenico, Playa la Ropa, Zihuatanejo ☎ (755) 555 7030

MAZATLÁN
♦♦ Hotel Azteca Inn ($$)
Friendly hotel. Well-furnished rooms with satellite TV, some overlooking pool. Bar, coffee shop, parking.

✉ Rodolfo T Loalza 307 ☎ (669) 913 1111

♦♦♦ Hotel Costa de Oro ($$)
Oceanside hotel with rooms arranged around inner patios, gardens, pool, and open-air restaurant. Tennis, tours.

✉ Camarón Sábalo, Zona Dorada ☎ (669) 913 5344

PUERTO VALLARTA
♦♦♦♦ Hacienda San Angel ($$$)
Romantic collection of three inter-connecting villas with nine suites. One villa, Casa Bursus, was Richard Burton's Puerto Vallarta home. Fantastic location.

✉ Miramar No. 336 ☎ (322) 222 2692

♦♦ Hotel Rosita ($$)
Vallarta's first hotel, overlooking main town beach, with clean, simple rooms. Good value for location.

✉ Paseo Diaz Ordaz 901 ☎ (322) 223 2000

RESTAURANTS

ACAPULCO
Carlos 'n Charlie's ($–$$)
This well-known resort chain serves decent food at reasonable prices. Lively atmosphere, loud rock music, and fast service.

✉ Costera Miguel Alemán 112, near the El Presidente Hotel ☎ (744) 484 1285 🕐 6pm–late

♦♦♦ Coyuca 22 ($$$)
Unique hilltop setting with fabulous bay views. Superlative international cuisine, professional service. Elegant dress required. Reservations essential.

✉ Carretera Las Brisas ☎ (744) 482 3468 🕐 Nov–Apr only

▼▼▼ El Ovido ($$)

Open, breezy restaurant on Acapulco Bay, with multi-tiered terraces among palm trees. Dishes relect a fusion of French and Mexican styles.

✉ Costera Miguel Alemán ☎ (744) 481 0214 🕙 6pm–midnight

MAZATLÁN
▼▼▼ El Parador Español ($–$$)

Spanish cuisine and seafood specialties. Popular, lively place with good service.

✉ Avenida Camarón Sábalo, next to El Cid ☎ (669) 983 0767
🕙 7am–midnight

Pancho's ($)

Locals in the know come to this bustling waterfront restaurant for breakfast where the *chilaquiles verdes con huevos* and the beautiful view are the perfect way to face the day ahead.

✉ Avenida Playa Las Gaviotas ☎ (669) 914 0911 🕙 7am–10pm

▼▼ El Shrimp Bucket ($$)

More fun in the evening when live marimba music enlivens the atmosphere. Mainly seafood; outdoor dining, great sea views.

✉ Olas Altas 11 ☎ (669) 981 6350 🕙 6am–11pm

▼▼ Senor Frog's ($–$$)

Part of the popular Mexican restaurant chain, serving a good selection of steaks, soups and well-prepared desserts. Gets very lively in the evenings.

✉ Avenida del Mar 882 ☎ (669) 985 1110 🕙 11am–1am

PUERTO VALLARTA
▼▼▼ La Palapa ($$)

Vallarta's original beachfront restaurant. Excellent seafood menu. Great position and ambience, candle-lit dinners.

✉ Calle Pulpito on Playa Los Muertos ☎ (322) 222 5225 🕙 Daily 8am–11pm

♦♦ Restaurant Argentino Los Pibes ($$$)

Steak restaurant, also serving delicious Thai and Chinese specialties include garlic shrimp, Changmai fish, and numerous vegetarian dishes.

✉ Basilio Badillo 261 ☎ (322) 223 1557 ⏰ 2pm–2am. Closed Sun

♦♦♦ Trio Restaurant ($$–$$$)

Fine European cuisine in a very popular dining spot, in the central part of the city. Live music and generous drinks.

✉ Guerrero 264 ☎ (322) 222 2196 ⏰ 6–11:30pm. Also noon–3:30 Nov–end Apr

SHOPPING

ART AND ANTIQUES

Galería Museo Huichol

Large gallery specializing in Huichol art and crafts, giving direct support to the crafts-people. Demonstrations.

✉ Morelos 490, Puerto Vallarta ☎ (322) 222 0182

Galería Uno

Contemporary art gallery in attractive converted house. Paintings, sculptures, graphics, and posters by well-known Mexican artists.

✉ Morelos 561, Puerto Vallarta ☎ (322) 222 0908 ⏰ Mon–Sat 10–8

Olinala Gallery

Well-displayed choice selection of fine indigenous art. Ritual masks, Huichol beadwork, lapidary work, and other rare original pieces.

✉ Lázaro Cárdenas 274, Puerto Vallarta ☎ (322) 222 4995 ⏰ Mon–Sat 10–2, 5–9pm

CLOTHING AND ACCESSORIES

Armando's

Light cotton women's jackets, dresses and other summerwear in tropical colors, often finely embroidered.

✉ Costera Miguel Alemán 1, Acapulco ☎ (744) 484 5111

Esteban's
Renowned local designer makes casual and evening wear for men and women to order. Ready-to-wear collection and accessories.
✉ Costera Miguel Alemán 2010, Acapulco ☎ (774) 484 3084

Gaby's Leather Factory
Understated-looking factory outlet offering good bargains in leather clothes and accessories for men and women. Custom fitting within the day.
✉ Camarón Sábalo 1652, Mazatlán ☎ (669) 916 1022

HANDICRAFTS
Origenes
A stylish interior design boutique with well-made furniture, basketware, lamps and ornaments. Great for special gifts.
✉ Calle Zaragoza 160, Puerto Vallarta ☎ (322) 223 1455 🕐 Daily 10–10

Quetzalcóatl
Spacious emporium of indigenous art such as beaded Huichol pieces, black pottery from Oaxaca, Aztec and Maya reproductions, masks and terracotta sculptures. Shipping can be arranged.
✉ Juárez 428, Puerto Vallarta ☎ (322) 223 2380 🕐 Mon–Sat 9:30–8:30

JEWELLERY
Albertós
This company has been designing and selling unique jewelry in gold, silver and precious stones since 1977.
✉ Calle Cuauhtémoc No 12 and No 15, Zihuatanejo ☎ (755) 554 2161

B & B Gold and Silver Factory
Supplier to many of Acapulco's other jewelry shops. Vast selection.
✉ Juan Sebastián El Cano 2, by Papagayo Park, Acapulco ☎ (744) 483 0441

Taxco Exporta
Wide selection of silver jewelry from Taxco, including some unique designs. Gold pieces and handicrafts too. Bargaining necessary.
✉ Calle La Quebrada 315 (opposite diving cliff), Acapulco ☎ (744) 482 7165

ENTERTAINMENT

NIGHTLIFE

Baby'O
Groundbreaking nightspot with dance floor surrounded by tiered spectator seats. Latest sound and light equipment, fast-paced.
✉ Costera Miguel Alemán 22, near Hyatt Regency, Acapulco ☎ (744) 484 7474 🕐 Daily 10pm–5am

Cactus
Spectacular and popular nightclub in Old Vallarta.
✉ Ignacio L Vallarta 399, Puerto Vallarta ☎ (322) 222 6037

Carlos n' Charlies
Typical resort chain restaurant with lively atmosphere, loud music, and dancing.
✉ Paseo del Palmar, next to Hotel Posada Real, Ixtapa ☎ (755) 553 0085

Club Christine
Classic mainstream disco with wide-ranging music.
✉ Hotel Krystal Vallarta, Zona Hotelera, Puerto Vallarta ☎ (322) 224 6990 🕐 Tue–Sun 10pm–4am

Collage
Entertainment center with billiards and backgammon, video games, sushi bar and dance floor.
✉ Calle Proa, at entrance to Marina Vallarta, Puerto Vallarta ☎ (322) 221 0505 🕐 Daily 11am–4am

La Valentina
More sophisticated than most, but still plenty of atmosphere.
✉ Boulevard Ixtapa, Ixtapa ☎ (755) 553 1190

Palladium
Popular nightspot, high on a hill. Glass walls give stunning bay views. Techno music dominates.
✉ Carretera Escénica Las Brisas, Acapulco ☎ (744) 446 5486

Salon Q

Hot tropical sounds keep the rhythm going in this huge dance spot with live bands. Salsa, cumbia, merengue and other Latin beats.

✉ Costera Miguel Alemán 23, near La Palapa, Acapulco ☎ (744) 481 0114

Zoo

Central Vallarta's most popular young nightspot, easily identified by the giraffe on its roof overlooking the bay. Techno, reggae, house, and disco music. Hard Rock Café is two doors away.

✉ Paseo Díaz Ordáz 630, Puerto Vallarta ☎ (322) 222 4945

SPORTS

Ecotours de Mexico

Kayaking, horseback riding, bird-watching, mountain biking, whale-watching, trekking.

✉ Ignacio L Vallarta 243, Puerto Vallarta ☎ (322) 222 6606/222 3310

Pacific Scuba

Diving (PADI certificates) includes night dives, snorkeling at Majahuita beach, Islas Marietas, and Los Arcos; whale-watching.

✉ Boulevard Francisco Medina Ascencio 2480, Puerto Vallarta ☎ (322) 209 0364

Vallarta Adventures

Cruises include snorkelling, kayaking, yoga, hiking, swimming with dolphins and lunch. Evening cruises include dinner.

✉ Paseo Las Palmas 39A, Puerto Vallarta ☎ (322) 221 0657

Yates del Sol

Speedboat and yacht rental, waterskiing, sunset cruises, snorkeling trips.

✉ Zihuatanejo ☎ (755) 554 2694

Zihuatanejo Scuba Center

Wide range of diving facilities from beginners to certification courses. Night dives. Marine biologist on call for specialists.

✉ Calle Cuauhtémoc 3, Zihuatanejo ☎ (755) 554 2147

The South

Indigenous people account for over 75 percent of the population in Southern Mexico, giving this region the look of authenticity. Beyond apparently deserted hills are villages with firmly entrenched customs and craft traditions.

Hugging the coast to the north is the state of Veracruz, land of riotous February carnivals and *marimba* bands that impart a distinctly tropical, almost Caribbean atmosphere. Oaxaca, to the south, remains queen of history, archaeology, culture, and crafts.

East of Veracruz is the oil-rich state of Tabasco, once the heart of Mesoamerica's oldest civilization, the Olmecs, but now clearly a front-runner in fast-developing Mexico.

Furthest south is the troubled state of Chiapas, where indigenous people have suffered at the hands of landowners and economic interests for centuries. This, too, is where high, pine-covered mountains alternate with tropical rainforests that conceal evocative Mayan ruins.

147

OAXACA

Oaxaca, capital of the state of the same name, is a graceful, small-scale city. Unique, colorful and full of surprises, it is one of Mexico's most relaxed, pleasurable towns. History is omnipresent yet not overpowering, while markets, art galleries, craft shops, cafés, and restaurants make for endless tempting distractions.

At Oaxaca's heart is the magnificent *zócalo,* rimmed by cafés, and a genuine crossroads for anyone in town. Once the center for the Mixtec and Zapotec civilizations, Oaxaca rapidly developed a strong Spanish flavor after it was conquered in 1533. Countless churches (including the masterful baroque Santo Domingo), elegant mansions, government buildings, decorative grille-work, and charming plazas were built, creating a harmonious backdrop for the strikingly proud indigenous population.

In 1987 Oaxaca, together with Monte Albán, a fabulous legacy of the Zapotecs (► 44–45) was declared a world heritage site by UNESCO. Excellent services, atmospheric hotels, and a network of craft villages have been organized and made accessible, offering a wide choice of activities to the visitor. The silhouette of Sierra Madre del Sur is a constant reminder of its rural attractions, whether on horseback, bicycle, or by car. However, Oaxaca's charm is best enjoyed on strolls along cobbled streets, past brightly painted houses, peeping into churches or courtyards, checking out shops, or people-watching on the *zócalo.*

Oaxaca endured months of political unrest in 2006, so check first whether it is safe to go (www.travel.state.gov.com).

✚ 18L

🛈 García Vigil 517 and Reforma 526

Museo de las Culturas de Oaxaca

Next door to Santo Domingo is the former Dominican monastery that now houses the regional museum, backed by a newly landscaped botanical garden. The rooms and vaulted cloisters of this building display the wealth of archaeological artifacts found in the state. Pride of place goes to the fantastic collection of Mixtec jewelry found in Tomb 7 at Monte Albán, including gold, turquoise, rock-crystal, jade, and silver.

✉ Ex-Convento de Santo Domingo, Alcalá ☎ (951) 516 2991 🕐 Tue–Sun 10–8 ✋ Moderate; free Sun

Museo Rufino Tamayo

The late Rufino Tamayo (1899–1991), one of Mexico's foremost 20th-century painters and a native of Oaxaca, spent over 20 years collecting pre-Hispanic antiquities, and this small, select museum is the result. Five color-coordinated rooms display some exceptional pieces, in particular those devoted to the Olmec, Occidente, Totonac, and Maya cultures.

Concerts and art exhibitions are also held here.

✉ Avenida Morelos 503 ☎ (951) 516 4750 🕐 Mon, Wed–Sat 10–2, 4–7, Sun 10–3 ✋ Inexpensive

a walk around Oaxaca

This walk through the colonial heart of Oaxaca takes in churches, museums, and the city's inimitable atmosphere.

Start at the zócalo and head for the Catedral on the north side.

Built in 1533, it contains a bronze altar, antique organ, and, best of all, an elaborate 18th-century baroque facade.

Leave the Catedral, turning sharply right, and walk along Independencia to the pedestrian street of Alcalá. Turn left and walk uphill to the Museo de Arte Contemporáneo. After visiting, continue uphill, turn right along Murguia as far as Cinco de Mayo, then turn left. On your right is the Camino Real Hotel.

This 400-year-old former convent of Santa Catalina, now a national monument, is very picturesque and exudes a distinctive atmosphere.

Continue uphill to Santo Domingo and visit both the church and adjacent museum. On leaving, turn right past the Instituto de Artes Gráficas to the Plazuela del Carmen Alto.

This small plaza is home to a colorful daily market of Oaxacan crafts.

Leave the plaza, turning left onto García Vigil. Continue downhill for four blocks before turning right into Morelos. Two blocks further is the Museo Rufino Tamayo. After visiting, continue another two blocks.

On the left is the Basílica de la Soledad, a late-17th-century church, home to a statue of the town's patron saint and a small museum.

Walk down the steps to Independencia. Turn left and walk four blocks east to the church of San Felipe Neri.

This church (1636) is noted for its fine frescoed walls and ornately gilded altar and nave.

Continue along Independencia to the zócalo.

Distance 2km (1 mile)
Time 3 hours including stops
Start/end point Zócalo
Lunch Café del Instituto de Artes Gráficas ($) ✉ Alcalá 507
❓ Check www.travel.state.gov.com for the latest on safety in Oaxaca

Templo de Santo Domingo

Started in the late 16th century, this is one of Mexico's finest examples of baroque architecture. Above the main entrance is an extraordinary bas-relief genealogical tree of the family of Domingo de Guzmán, the 13th-century founder of the Dominican order. Beyond this, the soaring ceiling is entirely faced in elaborately gilded and painted stucco, surrounding 36 inset paintings. To the right is the Capilla del Rosario, another magnificent interpretation of Mexican baroque by indigenous artisans.

✉ Alcalá, corner Gurrión 🕐 Mon–Sat 8–7:30, Sun 7–11, 1–7:30 💲 Free

More to see in the South

HUATULCO

Best places to see, pages 42–43.

MAZUNTE

This delightful, low-key fishing village lies 62km (39 miles) west of Huatulco, between Puerto Angel and Puerto Escondido. A beautiful adjoining beach, San Agustinillo, is popular with Mexicans for long lunches under shady *palapas*. Outlying rocks shelter the beach, making it ideal for those in search of calm waters and fresh seafood. Mazunte itself is home to the world's only turtle research center and the **Museo de la Tortuga,** an impressive modern set-up with turtles representing 9 of the world's 11 types. The wild 15km (9-mile) beach north of here, not accessible by road, sees the arrival of some 200,000 Olive Ridley turtles during their nesting season, from July to December. Mazunte is also home to a local enterprise making natural cosmetics.

✚ 18M

Museo de la Tortuga

✉ On main road (Mex 200) ☎ (958) 584 3055 🕐 Wed–Sat 10–4:30 ♨ Inexpensive 🍴 Excellent seafood restaurants ($) in Playa San Agustinillo

MITLA

Meaning "place of the dead," this fascinating
Zapotec site was occupied between AD400 and
700 but then became solely a ceremonial center.
Much of the rich stone-carving was finished by
the later Mixtecs, who alternated with the
Zapotecs in regional power until the Spanish
arrived in 1521. The structures are famed for their
complex geometrical stonework, made using an
inlay technique. This is particularly well preserved
in the Grupo de las Columnas, which contains the
masterful Patio de las Grecas. Nearby, another
patio structure incorporates two underground cruciform tombs.

The remains of Mixtec murals are displayed in the grounds of
the red-domed 16th-century church that rises above the site.
Behind it is a large crafts market. The village is dominated by small
crafts shops and *mezcal* bars, but don't miss the Frissell Museum,
on the plaza at the entrance.

✚ 19L ✉ Highway 190, 45km (28 miles) southeast of Oaxaca ⏱ Daily 8–5
💰 Inexpensive; free Sun

MONTE ALBÁN

Best places to see, pages 44–45.

PALENQUE

Best places to see, pages 48–49.

PUERTO ANGEL

This charming fishing port, nestling between forested hills, has
long been a favorite of those in the know. However, in 1997
Hurricane Pauline caused extensive damage, and although
reconstruction was rapid, some scars still remain.

There is little to do here except lap up the sun, lazing on the
pretty Playa Panteon and watching diving pelicans, but the slow

pace is appealing and the locals are extremely friendly. Ultra-fresh seafood is provided by fishermen who beach their boats or moor at the jetty. A short distance northwest is the hippie beach of Zipolite, where white sands ending in rocky headlands attract backpackers, while surfers revel in the often wild waves. Currents are dangerous and drownings have occurred.

✚ 18M ✉ 83km (52 miles) southeast of Puerto Escondido 🍴 Restaurant Susy ($), Playa del Panteon

PUERTO ESCONDIDO

Of the three beach resorts scattered along the Oaxacan coast, Puerto Escondido takes the middle road between sophisticated Huatulco (➤ 42–43) and relaxed Puerto Angel. Its fishing-village past has receded somewhat with the influx of hotels, restaurants and shops, but the lovely curved bay is only the beginning; to the east lie palm-fringed Playa Marinero and the surfers' paradise of Playa Zicatela, while to the west is the pretty cove of Puerto Angelito, accessible by boat or road. From Playa Principal a walkway winds around the cliffs, offering sweeping sea views. Nightlife thrives in the form of low-key beach bars.

✚ 18L ✉ 264km (164 miles) south of Oaxaca

ℹ Boulevard Benito Juárez s/n, Fraccionamento Bacocho ☎ (954) 582 0175

SAN CRISTÓBAL DE LAS CASAS

This beautiful but politically troubled town, high in the forested hills east of Tuxtla, remains a prime tourist favorite. Wood smoke fills the air in the narrow cobbled streets, shops offer an amazing array of local crafts, and hotels and restaurants are reasonable. Unfortunately, since the Zapatistas' uprising of 1994 events have proved that little is being done to improve rural conditions.

The main sights in town are the restored cathedral on the main square and, uphill on Avenida General Utrilla, the church of Santo Domingo (1547). Transformed in the 18th century, it presents a lacy, carved facade and an ornate baroque interior. Its terraces throng with an impromptu crafts market daily, while the adjoining monastery houses the **Centro Cultural de los Altos** and the weavers' co-operative, **Sna Jolobil.** The latter displays and sells examples of the skilled techniques still practised by local communities. Handicrafts continue two blocks north at the labyrinthine Mercado. East of here is Na-Bolom, a fascinating institution founded by Frans Blom and his wife Trudy. They both researched and supported local communities, leaving this house as a legacy to anthropologists and writers, who stay here.

San Cristóbal is also the starting point for excursions to local villages. San Juan Chamula, 9km (6 miles) north, has a large Sunday market in front of its extraordinary church. Here the Tzotzils carry on a form of worship that combines Christianity with ancient Mayan spiritual practices. Entry to the church is not allowed during religious ceremonies.

🔂 21L 🛈 Delegacion de Turismo, Avenida Miguel Hidalgo 2 ☎ (967) 678 6570/678 1467

Centro Cultural de los Altos

✉ Ex-Convento de Santo Domingo ☎ (967) 81609 🕔 Daily 10–5
✋ Inexpensive; free Sun

Sna Jolobil

✉ Ex-Convento de Santo Domingo ☎ (967) 678 2646 🕔 Mon–Sat 9–2, 4–6
✋ Free

TUXTLA GUTIÉRREZ

Although not an essential attraction in itself, Tuxtla is at the crossroads of several outstanding southern destinations. This modern capital of the state of Chiapas lies in a hot saucer rimmed by hills that rise in the east to San Cristóbal de las Casas. In the town center is the Parque Madero, a cultural complex containing a theater, botanic gardens, and the **Museo Regional,** which has a good display of Olmec and Mayan artifacts. To the south is a unique and enlightened zoo (➤ 71).

Chiapa de Corzo, 17km (10 miles) east on Highway 190, is the state's' first Spanish settlement, dating from 1528. The arcaded main square encloses a fountain structure, La Pila, built to resemble the Spanish crown. One block away is the vast church of Santo Domingo, whose former convent houses the Museo de la Laca (lacquer museum), a local craft specialty. Just behind flows the Río Grijalva. From the *embarcadero* (jetty) boats leave for tours of the Cañon de Sumidero. This canyon, with depths of over 1,000m (3,280ft), can also be viewed from lookout points along a road north of Tuxtla.

➕ 20L

🛈 Belisario Domínguez 950 ☎ (961) 602 5298

Museo Regional

✉ Parque Madero ☎ (961) 613 4479 🕓 Tue–Sun 9–4 ✋ Inexpensive; free Sun

VERACRUZ

Known above all for its riotous Shrovetide carnival, Veracruz was also the place where Hernán Cortés and his men first landed in 1519. This major port on the Gulf of Mexico later witnessed the arrival of French forces in 1838, and in 1847 was bombarded by the Americans. As a result, many of its monuments date from the late 19th century, with the exception of the beautiful **Fortaleza de San Juan de Ulua,** built in the 16th century and later much extended. Lying north of town in the main port area, the fort's sturdy walls and bastions, which once enclosed a political prison

and presidential palace, now contain a museum.

Life in central Veracruz revolves around the Plaza de Armas, flanked by the Catedral (1734) and the fine Palacio Municipal (1627), where hawkers vie with *marimba* bands long into the steamy night. The aquarium is also exceptional, but for swimming head south to the popular, though dirty, Mocambo beach, near Boca del Río.

➕ 19J

Fortaleza de San Juan de Ulua

✉ Islote de San Juan de Ulúa ☎ (228) 938 5151
🕓 Tue–Sun 9–5 🍴 Drinks available Expensive

VILLAHERMOSA

The modern, oil-rich city of Villahermosa is famed, above all, for its relics of the sophisticated Olmec civilization, Mesoamerica's oldest. A large leisure complex, the Centro de Investigaciones de las Culturas Olmecas (CICOM), includes exceptional Olmec pieces at its Museo de Antropología, but it is at the **Parque Nacional de La Venta** that you will see the impressive giant heads that were hauled here from their original site at La Venta, 95km (59 miles) away. These now sit in a lush, wooded area that also houses an excellent zoo of local Tabasco animals. More insights into local nature lie at Yumka, a well-organized 100ha (247-acre) jungle, savannah, and lagoon refuge for many endangered species (➤ 71).

✚ 21K

ℹ Avenue Los Rios y Calle 13 Tabasio 2000, 86035 Villahermosa ☎ (993) 316 3633/316 2889

Parque Nacional de La Venta

✉ Boulevard Adolfo Ruiz Cortines ☎ (933) 314 1652 🕓 Tue–Sat 9–4:30
♿ Inexpensive; free Sun 🍽 Cafeteria ($)

HOTELS

HUATULCO

▼▼▼ Crown Pacific Huatulco ($$$)

Lavish hotel built on a terraced hill overlooking Tangolunda Bay. Lots of steps, and some rooms are reached by funicular.

✉ Boulevard Benito Juarez 8, Bahía Tangolunda ☎ (958) 581 0044

OAXACA

▼▼▼▼ Camino Real Oaxaca ($$$)

Stunning 16th-century convent converted into a luxury hotel with colonnaded cloisters and a fountained courtyard. Rooms are airy, with high ceilings, bright decor and modern amenities.

✉ 5 de Mayo 300 ☎ (951) 501 6100

▼▼▼ Casa Oaxaca ($$$)

Superb eclectic hotel, decorated with exceptional contemporary Mexican taste. Spacious rooms and patios, pool, paintings. Breakfast included in very reasonable rates.

✉ García Vigil 407 ☎ (951) 514 4173

PALENQUE

▼▼ Chan-Kah Resort Village ($$$)

Beautifully sited *casitas* (bungalows) in lush jungle grounds very close to the arcaeological ruins. Good restaurant and *cenote*-type pool.

✉ Km3, Carretera a las Ruinas ☎ (916) 345 1100

SAN CRISTÓBAL DE LAS CASAS

Hotel Flamboyant Español ($$)

An elegant, colonial-style hotel with well-appointed rooms off flowery patio. Restaurant, bar, gym, solarium.

✉ Calle 1 de Marzo 15 ☎ (967) 678 0045

VERACRUZ

▼▼▼ ▼▼▼ Fiesta Americana Veracruz ($$$)

Beachside hotel in a modern commerical area, popular with businesspeople and families. Large airy rooms with luxurious bathrooms, kids' activities, restaurants.

✉ Boulevard Avila Camacho ☎ (229) 989 8989

VILLAHERMOSA
🍷🍷 Best Western Hotel Maya Tabasco ($$–$$$)
Small-scale hotel close to La Venta Park and the museums.
Comfortable air-conditioned rooms, pool, gym and restaurant.

✉ Boulevard Adolfo Ruiz Cortinez 907 ☎ (993) 358 1111

RESTAURANTS

HUATULCO
Oasis Café ($)
A popular spot on the main square. Seafood, grilled meats, salads,
sushi. Dine inside or out.

✉ Bugambilla, corner Flamboyant, La Crucecita ☎ (958) 587 0045

🕐 7am–midnight

OAXACA
Casa Oaxaca ($$$)
See page 58.

🍷🍷 El Asador Vasco ($$)
Out-of-this-world Mexican cuisine, with a touch of the continental.
Centrally located near the city's lively *zócalo*.

✉ Portal de Flores ☎ (951) 514 4755 🕐 1–11pm

🍷🍷 La Casa de la Abuela ($$)
Excellent regional specialties at a quaint hideaway. Classic
Oaxacan dining with a variety of *mole* sauces and crumbly white
Oaxacan cheese. Reservations suggested.

✉ Avenida Hidalgo 616 Altos ☎ (951) 516 3544 🕐 1–11pm

🍷🍷🍷 Restaurant El Naranjo ($$)
Courtyard restaurant close to the *zócalo*. Menu inspired by dishes
from all over Mexico. Specializes in *mole* dishes.

✉ Valerio Trujano 203, Col Centro ☎ (951) 514 1878 🕐 1–10pm

PUERTO ÁNGEL
Restaurant Susy ($)
Pleasant beachfront spot with tables under shady *palapas*. Ultra-fresh lobster, oysters, fish and ceviche, as well as generous fruit salads.

✉ Playa del Panteon ☎ (958) 584 0319

SAN CRISTÓBAL
Café La Selva ($)
Elegant coffee-house in contemporary style. Excellent coffee in all forms, snacks, cakes; newspapers.

✉ Avenida Cresencio Rosas, corner Cuauhtémoc ☎ (967) 678 7243

VILLAHERMOSA
💎💎 Los Tulipanes ($$)
Long-time local favorite overlooking a busy river. Features seafood and soups that integrate local herbs and spices – authentic Tabasco cuisine.

✉ Avenida Carlos Pellicer 511 ☎ (993) 312 9209 🕐 1–10pm

SHOPPING

ART AND ANTIQUES
Galería Gráfica Soruco
Interesting selection of works on paper, and photos.

✉ Plazuela Labastida 104C, Oaxaca ☎ (951) 514 3938

Galerías Huatulco
Contemporary works (paintings and sculptures) by artists from Oaxaca, Morelos, Michoacán and Jalisco. Also sells interesting jewelry designs in gold and silver.

✉ Hotel Sheraton, Tangolunda, Huatulco ☎ (958) 581 0080 🕐 Mon–Sat 9–1, 5–7, Sun 9–2

Galería Quetzalli
Large contemporary art gallery showing best of young Oaxacan artists. Combined with a bar-restaurant.

✉ Constitución 104, Oaxaca ☎ (951) 514 2606

La Mano Mágica
Long-established Oaxacan art gallery with regular exhibitions of contemporary artists and rug designs. Adjoining handicrafts store.
✉ Alcalá 203, Oaxaca ☎ (951) 516 4275

CLOTHES AND ACCESSORIES
Ay Caramba! Kanoa Boutique
Casual sportswear and beach clothing.
✉ Hotel Flamboyant, Plaza Principal, La Crucecita, Huatulco ☎ (958) 587 0244

Dishvé
A change from Oaxaca's indigenous embroidered clothes. Cheesecloth and cotton women's wear, some accessories. See next door too.
✉ Plaza Santo Domingo, Alcalá 407, Oaxaca ☎ (951) 514 2913

HANDICRAFTS
Instituto Oaxaqueno de las Artesanías
This government-run artists's co-operative sells work from around the state; there's a fine selection of painted copal-wood animals.
✉ Calle Garcia Vigil 809, Oaxaca ☎ (951) 514 2101

La Casa de la Iguana
Lizards are the central theme here, but they also sell many other unusual items from all over Mexico. Furniture and lamps too.
✉ Allende 109, Oaxaca ☎ (951) 516 0588

Mujeres Artesanas de las Regiones de Oaxaca
Sprawling showroom/store displaying craftswork by a local women's co-operative. Pottery, woodcarvings, weaving, embroidered clothes, leatherwork, and much more. Shipping.
✉ Calle 5 de Mayo 204, Oaxaca ☎ (951) 516 0670

JEWELRY
La Bodega del Fraile
Stocks an extensive selection of jewelry in a wide price range.

Monte Albán Mixtec replicas, Taxco silver, and more unusual local designs using semi-precious stones.

✉ Alcalá 501, Oaxaca ☎ (951) 516 4310

Jade Artesanias

Oaxacan handicrafts alongside replica jewelry and objects.

✉ García Virgil 703, Oaxaca ☎ (951) 516 0519

Oro de Monte Albán

Fabulous display of gold jewelry reproductions of the Mixtec hoard found at Monte Albán. This is one of several outlets.

✉ Alcalá 403, Oaxaca ☎ (951) 514 3813

Platería Maitl

Original designs in silver jewelry.

✉ Bugambillas 601C, La Crucecita, Huatulco ☎ (958) 587 1223

MARKETS

Mercado de Artesanías

Large crafts market southwest of the zócalo. Rugs, textiles, jewelry, painted wooden animals, and ceramics dominate. Bargaining essential.

✉ Zaragoza, corner J P García, Oaxaca 🕐 Daily 11–8

Mercado José Castillo Tielmans

The main indigenous market for surrounding villages. Fabulous crafts and ethnic variety.

✉ Avenida General Utrilla, corner Nicaragua, San Cristóbal de las Casas
🕐 Daily 6–3 (except Sun)

ENTERTAINMENT

NIGHTLIFE

Magic Circus Disco Club

Domed dance floor attached to Hotel Marlin at western end of Santa Cruz. Mainly international rock. Live bands.

✉ Andador Huatulco 102, Santa Cruz, Huatulco ☎ (958) 587 0017
🕐 Thu–Sat nights

Mágico Trópico

Live tropical and Latino music – *salsa* and more.

✉ Gardenia 311 Altos, opposite Hotel Flamboyant, Huatulco ☎ (958) 587 0702

Poison

Hip nightclub up a dirt road behind the marina. Partly open-air.

✉ Bahía de Santa Cruz, Huatulco ☎ (958) 587 1530

SPORTS

Centro de Buceo Curazao

A dive shop that also rents out diving gear and organizes trips. Handles windsurfing and sport fishing as well.

✉ Boca del Río, Veracruz ☎ (228) 822 2033

Community Museums of Oaxaca

Specialists in all types of eco-tours, including walking, horseback and bicycle trips.

✉ Constitució, Oaxaca ☎ (951) 516 2991

Eco-Discover Tours

Adventure trips round Huatulco's bays. Specializes in mountain biking and scuba diving but can also arrange horseback riding, kayaking and hiking.

✉ Plaza Las Conchas L-6, Tangolunda, Huatulco ☎ (958) 581 0002

Iguana Expediciones

Rafting, kayaking, and scuba diving in the Veracruz area.

✉ Cotaxtla Sur 16, Colonia Petrolera, Boca del Río, Veracruz ☎ (228) 821 1550

Jungle Tour

Quad bike (ATV) tours of the jungle around the reserves of Maguey and Organo Bays, with lunch on a beach.

✉ Lobby of Hotel Royal Maeva, Tangolunda, Huatulco ☎ (958) 581 0000

The Yucatán Peninsula

Jutting out between the Gulf of Mexico and the Caribbean is a flat limestone shelf riddled with underground rivers, caves and *cenotes* (sinkholes). Above ground this peninsula is less than inspiring, consisting mainly of monotonous savannah and low jungle. Yet it continues to attract charter-loads of visitors.

Mérida

The reason is quite simple; this was the heartland of the great Maya culture and, along with Guatemala, claims their most astonishing monuments. Chichén Itzá, Uxmal, Cobá, and Tulum, as well as many lesser-known sites, are a magnet for the historically inclined visitor. And beyond them lie the aquamarine depths of the Caribbean, where underwater life is hard to surpass. Lining the coast is a string of resorts, starting with Cancún, that cater for every touristic and hedonistic whim.

MÉRIDA

The elegant capital of the state of Yucatán makes a relaxed base for exploring major Mayan ruins such as Chichén Itzá (► 38–39)

and Uxmal (► 180). Mérida has a strong sense of history and culture, much of which has been absorbed from its links with the U.S., Cuba, Europe, and even the Middle East. This unusually cosmopolitan flavor expanded further in the 1950s when direct road and rail links were established with Mexico City.

When the Spaniards arrived in 1542, led by Francisco de Montejo, they used the stones of the declining Mayan city of T'ho to erect their cathedral and administrative structures. But it was not until the late 19th century that Mérida's fortunes really changed. The catalyst was the burgeoning sisal industry, whose prosperous French investors be-queathed an impressive *belle époque* architectural style. Today, many of the earlier colonial buildings around the *zócalo* have been restored, while to the north the tree-lined Paseo de Montejo is home to a string of grandiose edifices that were the residences of the sisal-empire builders. This area is now regarded as "modern" Mérida, characterized by airline offices, large hotels, and nightclubs.

South of the *zócalo*, in the streets surrounding the sprawling market, is a more mundane but authentic quarter, where everywhere you will see diminutive Mayan women in embroidered white dresses and older gentlemen in their immaculate white *guayaberas* (tucked shirts).

✚ 22H

🅹 Calle 59 No 514 ☎ (999) 930 3760

Casa de Montejo

This is Mérida's first Spanish house, built in 1549 by the conquistador Francisco de Montejo. His descendants lived there

until only a few years ago, but today the mansion more prosaically houses a branch of Banamex (bank). The facade is an outstanding example of the Plateresque style, with sculpted busts and the Montejo coat of arms depicting two soldiers triumphing over the bodies of prostrate Maya.

✉ Plaza Mayor, Calle 63

🕓 Mon–Fri 9–5 🎫 Free

🍴 Cafés and restaurants ($–$$) on square

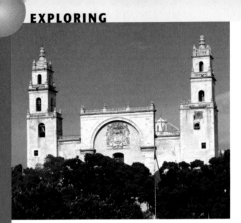

Catedral de San Ildefonso

Built between 1556 and 1599, this is said to be the oldest cathedral on the American continent, although Campeche's inhabitants would not agree. The massive edifice was built with the stones of the dismantled Mayan town of T'ho, but during the 1915 Revolution it was stripped bare. Today's worshippers venerate an impressive 7m-tall (23ft) statue of Christ that dominates the lofty stone interior. Other sights flanking the main square outside are the Palacio Municipal (1735) opposite, and the Palacio de Gobierno (1892) on the northern side, whose interior displays a remarkable series of 27 paintings depicting the complex history of the Maya, Spaniards, and Mexicans.

✉ Plaza Mayor, Calle 60 🕐 Daily 6am–7pm ✋ Free 🍴 Cafés and restaurants ($–$$) on square and along Calle 60

Museo de Antropología e Historia

Located on Mérida's most luxurious avenue, this elaborate 1911 mansion was built for the state governor to rival others belonging to prosperous sisal barons. As a result, the interior Doric columns, marble, chandeliers, and extravagant mouldings somewhat overpower the exhibits. These offer a clear background to the history of the Yucatán, its Mayan sites, and culture. Artifacts include a rare collection of jade offerings recovered from the cenote at Chichén Itzá.

✉ Palacio Canton, Paseo de Montejo 485 ☎ (999) 923 0557 🕐 Tue–Sat 8–8, Sun 8–2 ✋ Moderate; free Sun 🍴 Cafés and restaurants ($–$$) along Paseo de Montejo

More to see in the Yucatán Peninsula

CAMPECHE

Founded in the 1540s, Campeche suffered repeated attacks from pirates, and it was not until the erection of thick walls and eight bastions, in the late 17th century that it prospered. There are two excellent museums and several interesting churches, including the Catedral on the main square and the 16th-century church of San Francisco. In the central Baluarte de la Soledad is a superb display of Mayan stelae (carved stone slabs). A **museum** in the hilltop Fuerte de San Miguel has a rare collection of Maya jade and pottery.

✚ 22J

ℹ Avenida Ruiz Cortines s/n, Plaza Moch-Couoh ☎ (981) 811 9255

Museo Histórico Fuerte de San Miguel

✉ 4km (2.5 miles) south of Campeche 🕔 Tue–Sun 9–8, Sun 9–1

✋ Inexpensive

CANCÚN

Chosen by computer as the site of Mexico's largest resort in the early 1970s, Cancún attracts over 2.5 million visitors annually to indulge in powdery white-sand beaches, high-rise hotels, endless entertainment, sports and shopping. This is hardly the "real" Mexico, but makes an easy base for heading inland or further south along the increasingly developed "Maya Riviera." Most visitors come on package holidays and their 24-hour needs are well catered to. But long before the tourists came, there was a small Mayan settlement here. Its remains are visible at the Ruinas del Rey and at the **Museo Arqueológico.**

✚ 24H

🛈 Centro de Convenciones, KM 9, Boulevard Kukulcán ☎ (998) 884 6531

Museo Arqueológico

✉ Centro de Convenciones, Km 9, Boulevard Kukulcán A ☎ (998) 883 6671

🕓 Tue–Sun 8–7 ✋ Moderate; free Sun

CHICHÉN ITZÁ

Best places to see, pages 38–39.

COBÁ

This lakeside Mayan site remains little visited, despite its significance in the web of *sacbeob* (sacred "white paths") connecting other historic sites. Only a tiny proportion of this enormous city has been excavated, and these ruins are scattered through the jungle, so bring sturdy shoes, water, and insect repellent. Immediately visible is the Grupo de Cobá, whose narrow, steep pyramid rises over 30m (98ft) above the tree-tops to give sweeping views over the lake. A ball court is next on the trail, followed by the Conjunto de las Pinturas (Temple of the Painted Ladies), some carved stelae and altars known as the Grupo Macanxoc. Nearly 3km (2 miles) further on towers 42m-high (138ft) Nohoch Mul, the tallest pyramid in the northern Yucatán peninsula. A strenuous climb is rewarded by a small temple decorated with descending god figures.

✚ 24H ✉ 42km (26 miles) northwest of Tulum ☎ (98) 324634 🕓 Daily 7am–6pm ✋ Moderate; free Sun 🍴 Cafés and restaurants ($)

a drive from Cancún to Cobá

This drive takes you inland from Cancún to the colonial town of Valladolid and the Mayan site of Cobá. A dip in a *cenote* is an option.

Drive west out of Cancún along Avenida López Portillo following signs for Valladolid/Mérida. Avoid the cuota highway (a pricey tollroad, though quicker) and remain on the old Highway 180 which takes you through a string of pretty rural villages.

Traditional Mayan houses are generally elliptical in shape with tightly aligned tree-branch walls and *palapa* (thatched palm-leaf) roofs.

Drive 159km (99 miles) to Valladolid, watching out for the countless topes (speed bumps) that pepper every village. Drive straight into Valladolid's main plaza then follow Calle 41 west for two blocks, where it forks. Go left (Calle 41a) for another three blocks.

In front of you stands the bright yellow San Bernardino de Siena, a 16th-century Franciscan church and monastery. Often targeted by indigenous rebellions, the interior is practically bare.

Continue southwest a few blocks to the Cenote Dzitnup, signposted on the outskirts.

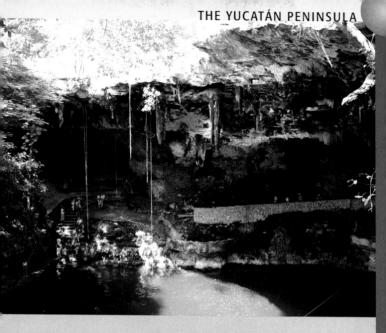

Have a refreshing dip in this beautiful *cenote* before returning to the main plaza. Park, visit the church of San Servacio, shop, then have lunch.

Drive back 28km (17 miles) along Highway 180 to Chemax and turn right to Cobá. Another 30km (19 miles) brings you to this archaeological site (➤ 173). Leave Cobá by following signs to Tulúm, then watch for a turn-off to the left after a few kilometers/miles. This brings you to Tres Reyes and back to Highway 180 or the toll road to Cancún.

Distance 350km (217 miles)
Time 9–10 hours (including stops)
Start/end point Avenida López Portillo, Cancún ✚ 24H
Lunch Hotel María de la Luz ($) ✉ Plaza Principal, Valladolid
☎ (985) 856 2071

COZUMEL

Like Cancún, the island of Cozumel is almost entirely geared to the needs of tourists. Cruise ship passengers, scuba divers and Cancunites all come to taste the delights of the renowned Palankar Reef, one of the world's top diving destinations. Unfortunately the most visited beach, Chankanab, now offers mainly dead coral, although the fish are spectacular. Skilled divers make day trips to some 20 different sites further out. Good swimming beaches dot the southwestern corner of the island, but strong currents make the eastern coast dangerous. In the unspoiled north lies a late Mayan site, **San Gervasio,** with a temple dedicated to Ixchel, goddess of fertility. The main town, San Miguel, is a modernized place, where, again, the flavor of real Mexico is virtually absent.

✚ 24H

ℹ Plaza del Sol, in the *zócalo* ☎ (987) 869 0211

San Gervasio

✉ 13km (8 miles) northeast of San Miguel ☎ (987) 800 2215 🕐 Daily 7–5
🚢 Frequent ferries from Playa del Carmen, boat trips from Cancún

GRUTAS DE LOLTÚN

These spectacular underground caves and galleries lie in the heart of the undulating Puuc Hills, south of Mérida. Inhabited over 2,500 years ago, their secret network was also used by rebellious Maya seeking refuge during the mid-19th-century Caste War. Fabulous rock formations, cave paintings, musical stalactites and the Cathedral, a large chamber that soars over 50m (164ft) high, are all part of this compelling underworld.

✚ 23J ✉ 115km (71 miles) south of Mérida, 50km (31 miles) east of Uxmal 🕐 Daily guided tours at 9:30, 11, 12:30, 2, 3:30 👊 Moderate
🍴 Café ($) at entrance

ISLA MUJERES

This delightful little island has a sleepy rhythm of its own. Most streets are of sand, cars are outnumbered by golf-carts and bicycles, and nights are tranquil. It makes an enticing escape from the over-development on Cancún, and as well as good beaches and diving, offers several attractions. The main town and services adjoin Playa Norte, while at the far southern tip is **El Garrafón,** a national park covering part of the Great Mayan Reef. Although the coral is dead, boat trips take snorkelers and divers to better spots further afield.

Half-way down the central lagoon lies Dolphin Discovery, a registered dolphin center, near a turtle farm. A small altar to the fertility goddess Ixchel explains the island's name (island of women); when the Spanish first landed they found numerous crude statues of her. Day trips also go to Isla Contoy (➤ 72), an uninhabited bird sanctuary.

➕ 24H

ℹ️ Rueda Medina, opposite jetty ☎ (998) 877 0307

Parque Nacional El Garrafón

✉️ Carretera al Faro ☎ (998) 877 1100 🕐 Daily 8:30–6:30 Expensive 🍴 Snack bar ($) on terrace

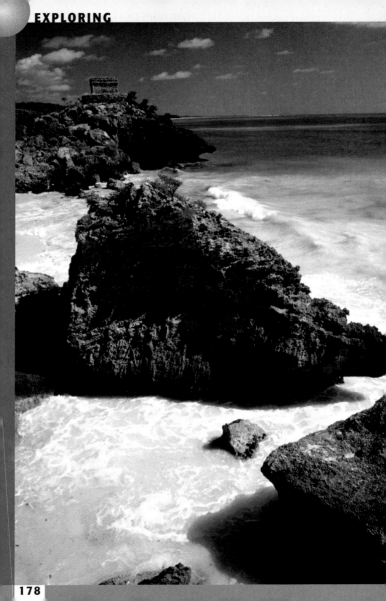

PLAYA DEL CARMEN

Once a beach-bum's paradise, this small resort is mushrooming fast. The modern town center is built on a narrow grid of streets bisected by Avenida 5, a favorite promenading and restaurant strip, ending at palm-fringed Caribbean beaches. South of the Cozumel ferry pier is an airstrip and golf course, while north of town hotels are rapidly eating up the shore. Nightlife, eating, and shopping opportunities are plentiful, but there is little else.

✚ 24H ☎ Free info-line 1-800-GO-PLAYA

TULÚM

This dramatically situated Mayan ruin (AD900–1500) rises perilously on a cliff edge north of a slowly expanding stretch of hotels. Inland lies a typical services town without much beauty but with reasonable prices. However, if you want a few quiet days of sleeping beside the waves, Tulum's beach accommodation is ideal.

The ruins themselves are now fronted by a large shopping plaza from where a tram ferries visitors to the site, although it is within easy walking distance. Sadly, this new structure has taken away much of Tulum's drama, but the Templo de los Frescos is still remarkable for its faded interior murals, the palace for its carved figures, and the Castillo complex for its serpentine columns and sweeping sea views.

✚ 24J ✉ Highway 307 🕐 Daily 8–5 💰 Moderate; free Sun 🍴 Snack bars ($) in plaza

UXMAL

Uxmal was founded between the 5th and 6th centuries AD and at one point had some 25,000 inhabitants, before being abandoned around 900. It stands on a wide plateau in the Puuc Hills, near several smaller sites of similar style. Outstanding is the Pirámide del Adivino (Magician's Pyramid), an elliptical structure rising over 40m (130ft) high. Immediately to the west stands the Cuadrángulo de las Monjas (The Nuns' Quadrangle), where fine stone inlay typifies the Puuc style. South of here is an elevated complex, the Palacio del Gobernador (Governor's Palace) showing unsurpassed decorative techniques. Beyond is the Casa de las Tortugas (House of the Turtles), the Gran Pirámide (Great Pyramid), and the Casa de la Vieja (Old Lady's House). Visitors with guides can see the last two structures where numerous sculpted phalluses at the Templo de los Falos (Temple of Phalluses) point to a unique cult in Uxmal.

✚ 22J ✉ 78km (48 miles) south of Mérida on Highway 261 🕒 Daily 8–5
🍴 Restaurant ($) in museum complex ✋ Expensive; moderate Sun
❓ Spectacular sound-and-light show at 7pm in Spanish, 9pm in English

HOTELS

CANCÚN
◈◈◈◈ Hilton Cancun Beach and Golf Resort ($$$)
Dramatic pyramid building with extensive pool areas. All rooms have views of the Caribbean. 18-hole golf course.
✉ Boulevard Kukulcán Km 17 ☎ (998) 881 8000

◈◈ Sunset Lagoon Hotel & Marina ($$–$$$)
Mediterranean-style architecture, patios, gardens facing Laguna de Nichupté; some rooms with whirlpools. Great for watersports and close to the shopping malls in the heart of the Hotel Zone.
✉ Boulevard Kukulcán Km 5.8 ☎ (998) 881 4500

CHICHÉN ITZÁ
◈◈ Hacienda Chichén Resort ($$$)
Lovely 16th-century hacienda hotel with modern air-conditioned cottage accommodation. Beautiful gardens, pool, restaurant.
✉ Chichén Itzá ☎ (985) 851 0045

COZUMEL
◈◈ Playa Azul Hotel ($$$)
Small-scale hotel toward the northern end of the island. Rooms overlook a secluded beach or gardens. Close to town.
✉ Carretera San Juan Km4 ☎ (987) 872 0199

ISLA MUJERES
◈ Hotel Na Balam ($$)
Lovely beach hotel in sophisticated palapa style. Standard rooms have king- or queen-size beds. Tropical garden with hammocks under palm trees, yoga, pool, bar and restaurant.
✉ Calle Zazil Ha 118 ☎ (998) 877 0279

MÉRIDA
◈ Hotel Caribe ($)
Central hotel with a quaint colonial atmosphere, ideal for touring the city. Rooms are basic but clean, most with air-conditioning.
✉ Calle 59 No 500 ☎ (999) 924 9022

♦♦ Hotel Casa del Balam ($$$)

Stylish central hotel in modernized 19th-century building. Soundproofing, pool, colonial features, satellite TV, travel agency, parking.

✉ Calle 60 No 488 ☎ (999) 924 8844

PLAYA DEL CARMEN
♦♦ Caribbean Paradise ($$–$$$)

Small-scale hotel, decorated in Mexican style, with great views of the Caribbean and the town. Air-conditioned rooms have balcony or terrace.

✉ Avenida 5 ☎ (984) 803 2032

TULUM
♦♦♦ Copa Cabana Beach Resort ($$$)

Large, all-inclusive resort featuring lavish public areas, modern rooms, excellent service and wide beach on the Caribbean. Some rooms have whirlpools.

✉ Carretera Cancun–Chetumal ☎ (984) 875 1800

UXMAL
♦♦♦ The Lodge at Uxmal ($$$)

Blends Mayan and European architectural styles. Two pools, plus views of Uxmal. The restaurant serves Mexican, Yucatecan and international cuisine.

✉ At the main entrance to the archaeological site ☎ (987) 976 2031

RESTAURANTS

CAMPECHE
Restaurant Miramar ($$)

One of Campeche's best seafood restaurants, near the port.

✉ Calle 8 y 61 ☎ (981) 816 2883 🕐 Daily 11–3, 6–10:30

CANCÚN
♦♦♦ Los Almendros ($)

Classic Yucatecan fare such as *cochinita pibil* (pork baked in a banana leaf). Live trio music in evening. In downtown area.

✉ Avenida Bonampak, corner Avenida Sayil ☎ (798) 887 1332
🕐 10am–11pm

♦♦ Captain's Cove ($$)

Palapa restaurant overlooking lagoon. Ultra-fresh seafood specialties, barbecued meats and Mexican dishes. Happy hour 4–7pm.

✉ Boulevard Kukulcán, Km 9.5 ☎ (998) 885 0016 🕐 Daily 2–11pm

♦♦♦ La Dolce Vita ($$$)

Excellent Italian cuisine: fresh pasta, seafood, salads. Attentive service. Booking advisable.

✉ Boulevard Kukulcán, Km 14.6, opposite Hotel Marriott ☎ (998) 885 0161
🕐 Lunch and dinner

COZUMEL
♦♦ La Choza ($–$$)

Simple, family-run palapa serving traditional Yucatecan cooking. A fun and casual experience.

✉ Avenida 10 Sur ☎ (987) 872 0958 🕐 7:30am–10:30pm

ISLA MUJERES
♦ Zazil-Ha ($$$)

Romantic outdoor setting in hotel garden. Wide-ranging menu includes salads, seafood, pasta, and meat dishes. Good bar with 7–9pm happy hour.

✉ Calle Zazil-Ha 118, Playa Norte ☎ (998) 877 0279 🕐 Daily 7:30am–10pm

MÉRIDA
♦♦ Los Almendros ($$)

Famous Yucatecan restaurant. Fine choice of local specialties; regional show on Fridays at 7.

✉ Calle 50-A No 493, Plaza de la Mejorada ☎ (999) 923 8135 🕐 Daily 9am–11pm

♨♨ La Parrilla ($–$$)

Lively restaurant in the historic downtown area serving a wide assortment of Yucatecan specialties.

✉ Calle 60 esq con Calle 59 ☎ (999) 944 3999 🕓 11am–midnight; Fri–Sat until 2am

SHOPPING

CLOTHING AND ACCESSORIES

Qué Barbara

Unusual designs from Guatemala, mainly for women.

✉ Calle Matamoros 18, Isla Mujeres ☎ (987) 877 0705

MARKET

Mercado Municipal de Artesanías

A sprawling crafts market in two separate buildings. Mayan embroidered dresses, lace, hammocks, sea shells, Panama hats. Prices are exorbitant and demand hard bargaining.

✉ Calle 65, corner Calle 56, behind post office, Mérida 🕓 Daily 9–5

ENTERTAINMENT

NIGHTLIFE

La Boom

This is one of Cancún's favorite night spots. Vast disco and adjacent bar, live rock music.

✉ Paseo Kukulcán, near bridge, Cancún ☎ (998) 849 7588

Cancún Queen

Enjoy a paddle-steamer cruise through the mangroves of Nichupté Lagoon with three-course dinner, live band, dancing, and games.

✉ Aquaworld, Boulevard Kukulcán 15, Cancún ☎ (998) 885 5228 🕓 Daily at 6:30pm

Carlos n' Charlies

Something of a Cancún legend, this is the type of joint where the staff often join the band on stage and the conga line just grows.

✉ Boulevard Kukulcán Km 5.5, Cancún ☎ (998) 849 4053 🕓 Daily noon–5am

Dady'O

Gigantic and legendary disco with tiered seating, blinding laser shows, and mainly techno rhythms.

✉ Km 9.5, Paseo Kukulcán, Cancún ☎ (998) 883 3333 🕐 Daily from 10pm

Mango Tango

Caribbean exuberance in nightly floor show and sounds.

✉ Boulevard Kukulcán 14.2, opposite Ritz-Carlton Hotel, Cancún ☎ (998) 885 0303 🕐 Dinner show starts at 8pm daily

Pat O'Brian's

An offspring of the well-known New Orleans bar. Lagoon view, generous drinks, outrageous setting and lots of live piano.

✉ Plaza Flamingo, Cancún ☎ (998) 883 0832 🕐 Daily 11am–12:30am

SPORTS

Coral Scuba Dive Center

Scuba diving trips, snorkeling.

✉ Avenida Matamoros 13A, Isla Mujeres ☎ (998) 877 0371

Diving Adventures

Scuba diving school, full PADI certificates. Daily boat dives for all levels. Nitrox dives available.

✉ Calle 5 No 2, San Miguel, Cozumel ☎ (987) 872 3009

Solo Buceo

Scuba diving and snorkeling training and accompanied dives.

✉ Boulevard Kuklacán – Punta Cancún, Cancún ☎ (998) 884 7070

Tak-Be-Ha

Cavern diving, cave and cenote snorkeling, jungle treks.

✉ Highway 307, just south of Xel-Ha, near Tulum ☎ (984) 877 8535
🕐 Tours daily 9am, 11am, 1pm

Index

Acknowledgements

The Automobile Association would like to thank the following photographers, companies and picture libraries for their assistance in the preparation of this book.

Abbreviations for the picture credits are as follows – (t) top; (b) bottom; (c) centre; (l) left; (r) right; (AA) AA World Travel Library.

4l Taxco, AA/R Strange; **4c** Teotihuacán, AA/R Strange; **4r** Lake Arareco, AA/F Dunlop; **5l** Guadalupe, AA/R Strange; **5r** Guanajuato, AA/C Sawyer; **6/7** Taxco, AA/R Strange; **8/9** Horse, AA/C Sawyer; **10cl** Tiled building, AA/C Sawyer; **10/lt** traditional hat, AA/C Sawyer; **10/1c** Day of the Dead papier mache figure, AA/R Strange; **10br** Mariachi, AA/C Sawyer; **11tr** Puebla, AA/C Sawyer; **11tcr** Xilitla, AA/R Strange; **11bcr** Loreto, AA/L Dunmire; **11br** El Tajin, AA/R Strange; **12/3t** Street vendors, AA/C Sawyer; **12/3b** Food, AA/C Sawyer; **13t** Barmen, AA/C Sawyer; **14** Restaurant, AA/C Sawyer; **15bl** Tequila, AA/R Strange; **15tr** Fish Market, AA/R Strange; **15cr** Alcoholic drinks, AA/C Sawyer; **15br** Mezcal, AA/R Strange; **16** Cathedral, AA/C Sawyer; **16/7** Puerto Vallarta, AA/R Strange; **17t** Macaw, AA/R Strange; **17b** Lake Patzcuaro, AA/R Strange; **18** Scuba diving; AA/R Strange; **18/9** Market, AA/C Sawyer; **19tr** Flower Seller, AA/R Strange; **19br** Chichén Itzá, AA/R Strange; **19bl** Artefact, AA/R Strange; **20/1** Teotihuacan, AA/R Strange; **24/5** Pilgrims, AA/R Strange; **26** Cruise Liner, AA/L Dunmire; **27** Bus, AA/C Sawyer; **30** Telephone, AA/L Dunmire; **31** Sign, AA/R Strange; **32** Policeman, AA/C Sawyer; **34/5** Lake Arareco, AA/F Dunlop; **36** Batopilas, AA/ F Dunlop; **36/7** Batopilas, AA/F Dunlop; **38/9t** Chichén Itzá, AA/R Strange; **38/9b** Chichén Itzá, AA/R Strange; **40** Guanajuato, AA/C Sawyer; **40/1** Guanajuato, AA/C Sawyer; **41t** Museo de las Momias, AA/R Strange; **42** Beach at Tangolunda in Huatulco, AA/C Sawyer; **42/3** Huatulco, AA/C Sawyer; **44/5** Monte Alban, AA/R Strange; **45** Monte Alban, AA/R Strange; **46/7** Museo Nacional de Antropologia, AA/C Sawyer; **48** Palenque, AA/C Sawyer; **48/9** Palenque, AA/C Sawyer; **50/1** Taxco, AA/R Strange; **51** Taxco, AA/C Sawyer; **52** Teotihuacán, AA/C Sawyer; **52/3t** Teotihuacán, AA/R Strange; **52/3b** Teotihuacán, AA/R Strange; **54/5** Xochimilco, AA/R Strange; **56/7** Guadalupe, AA/R Strange; **59** Restaurant, AA/C Sawyer; **60/1** Golf, AA/C Sawyer; **62/3** Yagul, AA/S Watkins; **64/5** Puebla, AA/C Sawyer; **66/7** Queretaro, AA/C Sawyer; **68/9** Janitzio, AA/C Sawyer; **70/1** CICI, AA/C Sawyer; **71** Bosque de Chapultepec, AA/C Sawyer; **72/3** Sierra de la Giganta, AA/L Dunmire; **74/5** Loreto, AA/L Dunmire; **76/7** Guanajuato, AA/C Sawyer; **79** Children playing, AA/C Sawyer; **80** Palacio Nacional, AA/C Sawyer; **80/1** Bosque de Chapultepec, AA/C Sawyer; **82** Museo Anahuacalli, AA/R Strange; **82/3** Cathedral, AA/C Sawyer; **84** San Angel, AA/C Sawyer; **84/5** San Angel, AA/C Sawyer; **86/7** Museo Frida Kahlo, AA/C Sawyer; **87** Palacio de bellas Artes, AA/P Wilson; **88** Palacio Nacional, AA/C Sawyer; **88/9** Templo Mayor, AA/R Strange; **90** Cholula, AA/R Strange; **90/1** Mariachis, AA/C Sawyer; **92/3** Guadalajara, AA/R Strange; **94** Jalapa, AA/P Wilson; **94/5** Laguna de Chapala, AA/R Strange; **96/7** Patzcuaro, AA/C Sawyer; **97** Puebla, AA/C Sawyer; **98** Patzcuaro, AA/C Sawyer; **98/9** Janitzio, AA/C Sawyer; **100** Queretaro, AA/C Sawyer; **101** El Tajin, AA/R Strange; **113** Ensenada, AA/L Dunmire; **114** Chihuahua Pacifico railroad, AA/P Wilson; **114/5** Casas Grande, AA/P Wilson; **115** Chihuahua, AA/P Wilson; **116/7** Ensenada, AA/P Wilson; **117** Hermosillo, AA/P Wilson; **118/9** La Paz, AA/L Dunmire; **120** Los Cabos, AA/L Dunmire; **121** Todos Santos, AA/L Dunmire; **122/3t** Loreto, AA/L Dunmire; **122/3b** Loreto, AA/L Dunmire; **124/5** Museo de Mulege, AA/L Dunmire; **125** San Ignacio, AA/L Dunmire; **131** Puerto Vallarta, AA/P Wilson; **132** Acapulco, AA/C Sawyer; **132/3** CICI, AA/C Sawyer; **133** Acapulco, AA/C Sawyer; **134/5** La Quebrada, AA/R Strange; **135** View to Isla Ixtapa, AA/ R Strange; **136/7** Puerto Vallarta, AA/R Strange; **138** Puerto Vallarta, AA/R Strange; **139** Puerto Vallarta, AA/R Strange; **147** Local people, AA/C Sawyer; **148** Oaxaca, AA/R Strange; **148/9** Oaxaca, AA/R Strange; **149** Rufino Tamayo Museum, AA/R Strange; **150** Rufino Tamayo Museum, AA/R Strange; **150/1** Oaxaca, AA/R Strange; **152/3** Oaxaca, AA; **153** Huatulco, AA/C Sawyer; **154** Mitla, AA/S Watkins; **155** Puerto Escondido, AA/C Sawyer; **156/7** Balloon seller, AA/C Sawyer; **158** Canon de Sumidero, AA/R Strange; **158/9** Musicians, AA/C Sawyer; **160** Villahermosa, AA/R Strange; **167** Fishing Boat, AA/R Strange; **168** Merida, AA/C Sawyer; **168/9t** Merida, AA/R Strange; **169b** Casa de Montejo, AA/C Sawyer; **170** Cathedral, AA/C Sawyer; **170/1** Campeche, AA/C Sawyer; **172** Cancun, AA/C Sawyer; **174** Coba, AA/R Strange; **175** Valladolid, AA/C Sawyer; **176/7t** Cozumel, AA/R Strange; **176/7b** Isla Mujeres, AA/C Sawyer; **178** Tulum, AA/P Wilson; **179** Playa del Carmen, AA/C Sawyer; **180** Uxmal, AA/R Strange.

Every effort has been made to trace the copyright holders, and we apologise in advance for any accidental errors. We would be happy to apply the corrections in the following edition of this publication.

Sight locator index

This index relates to the maps on the cover. We have given map references to the main sights in the book. Some sights may not be plotted on the maps.

Questionnaire

Dear Traveler

Your comments, opinions and recommendations are very important to us. So please help us to improve our travel guides by taking a few minutes to complete this simple questionnaire.

Send to: Essential Guides,
MailStop 64, 1000 AAA Drive, Heathrow, FL 32746–5063

Your recommendations...

We always encourage readers' recommendations for restaurants, nightlife or shopping – if your recommendation is added to the next edition of the guide, we will send you a FREE AAA Essential Guide of your choice. Please state below the establishment name, location and your reasons for recommending it.

_____

_____

_____

_____

Please send me AAA Essential _____

About this guide...

Which title did you buy?

_____ **AAA Essential**

Where did you buy it? _____

When? m m / y y

Why did you choose a AAA Essential Guide? _____

_____

_____

Did this guide meet with your expectations?

Exceeded ☐   Met all ☐   Met most ☐   Fell below ☐

Please give your reasons _____

_____

_____

continued on next page...

Were there any aspects of this guide that you particularly liked? _____

_____

_____

_____

_____

Is there anything we could have done better? _____

_____

_____

_____

_____

About you…
Name (Mr/Mrs/Ms) _____

Address _____

_____ **Zip** _____

Daytime tel nos. _____

Which age group are you in?
Under 25 ☐   25–34 ☐   35–44 ☐   45–54 ☐   55–64 ☐   65+ ☐

How many trips do you make a year?
Less than one ☐   One ☐   Two ☐   Three or more ☐

Are you a AAA member?   Yes ☐   No ☐
Name of AAA club _____

About your trip
When did you book? m m / y y   **When did you travel?** m m / y y

How long did you stay? _____

Was it for business or leisure? _____

Did you buy any other travel guides for your trip?   Yes ☐   No ☐
If yes, which ones? _____

Thank you for taking the time to complete this questionnaire.